A Reader's Guide to Reformed Literature

An Annotated Bibliography of Reformed Theology

Joel R. Beeke

REFORMATION HERITAGE BOOKS
Grand Rapids, Michigan

Copyright © 1999
Reformation Heritage Books
2919 Leonard St., NE, Grand Rapids, MI 49525
616-977-0599/Fax 616-977-0889/e-mail jrbeeke@aol.com
website: www.heritagebooks.org
ISBN 1-892777-15-0

All rights reserved. Printed in the United States of America.

For additional volumes of Reformed persuasion, both new and used, request a free book list from the above address.

Table of Contents

ARTICLE 1	The Doctrine of God	1
ARTICLE 2	By What Means God is Made Known Unto Us	3
ARTICLE 3	The Inspiration of the Scriptures	6
ARTICLE 4	The Canon of the Scriptures	8
ARTICLE 5	The Authority of Scripture	10
ARTICLE 6	The Apocrypha	12
ARTICLE 7	Scripture's Sufficiency and Inerrancy	14
ARTICLES 8-9	The Trinity	16
ARTICLE 10	The Deity of Jesus Christ	19
ARTICLE 11	The Deity of the Holy Spirit	22
ARTICLE 12	Creation, Angels, and Devils	24
ARTICLE 13	Divine Providence	27
ARTICLE 14	Our Creation, Fall, and Bound Will	30
ARTICLE 15	Original Sin	34
ARTICLE 16	Predestination: Election and Reprobation	36
ARTICLE 17	God Promises Salvation in Christ to Fallen Man	40
ARTICLE 18	The Incarnation	43
ARTICLE 19	Christ's Two Natures in One Person	45
ARTICLE 20	Justice and Mercy in Christ	47
ARTICLE 21	Salvation in Christ as High Priest	50
ARTICLE 22	Salvation by Faith in Christ Alone	53
ARTICLE 23	Justification	56
ARTICLE 24	Sanctification and Holiness	60
ARTICLE 25	The Ceremonial Law	62

ARTICLE 26	Christ's Intercession	65
ARTICLE 27	The Doctrine of the Church	67
ARTICLE 28	Church Membership	70
ARTICLE 29	The True and the False Church Compared	72
ARTICLE 30	Church Government and Offices	74
ARTICLE 31	Ministers, Elders, and Deacons	76
ARTICLE 32	Church Order, Worship and Discipline	80
ARTICLE 33	The Sacraments	83
ARTICLE 34	Holy Baptism	85
ARTICLE 35	The Holy Supper	88
ARTICLE 36	Church and State	91
ARTICLE 37	The Last Judgment; Hell and Heaven	94

Sources for Reformed Literature 97

PREFACE

This book provides a basic annotated bibliography of the most important books of Reformed theology. I have divided the bibliography into 36 sections that correspond with the titles of the articles of the Belgic Confession of Faith. The Belgic Confession (1561), written primarily by Guido de Brès, masterfully summarizes Reformed theology. For people who are unfamiliar with Reformed theology, I have provided suggestions at the end of most sections as to where to begin reading.

This bibliography was originally published with a series of articles in *Christian Observer*. It is also included in *Reformed Confessions Harmonized,* a parallel harmony of the seven major Reformed confessions used today (edited by Sinclair Ferguson and myself and published by Baker Book House, Grand Rapids).

I thank Iain Murray, Ray Lanning, and Susan Freeland for their suggestions and proofreading; Phyllis TenElshof for editing; Gary and Linda den Hollander for typesetting; Karl VanOostenbrugge for cover photography; Samuel Van Grouw, Jr. for the cover design; and my wife Mary for her patience with my love for Reformed literature. It is my hope that this bibliography will prompt many to further study of Reformed theology.

—JRB

ARTICLE 1

The Doctrine of God

The classic work on God's undeniable existence and attributes is Stephen Charnock's (1628-1680) fourteen massive *Discourses on the Existence and Attributes of God* (1682; reprint 2 vols., Grand Rapids: Baker, 1979). *Discourses* is marked by sound Puritan theology, profound thought, and humble adoration of God. Charnock intended to preach an entire "body of divinity," but he came no further than the attributes of God before being taken into the very presence of God at the age of fifty-two.

Another significant Puritan work on God's attributes is William Bates (1625-1699), *The Harmony of the Divine Attributes in the Contrivance and Accomplishment of Man's Redemption* (1674; reprint Harrisonburg, VA: Sprinkle, 1985). Bates focuses on God's justice, holiness, power, and mercy. He stresses practical piety and is a master of the Puritan "plain style" of preaching.

Two nineteenth-century works are quite helpful: Robert Phillip, *The Eternal; or, The Attributes of Jehovah* (London: Ward, 1846), and Alexander Carson, *The Knowledge of Jesus the Most Excellent of the Sciences* (New York: Edward Fletcher, 1851). Carson's volume is misnamed; it contains a classic presentation of God's attributes with little focus on Christ until the last chapter.

Standard Reformed dogmatics often have valuable sections on the doctrine of God. Herman Hoeksema, *Reformed Dogmatics* (Grand Rapids: Reformed Free, 1966) is particularly moving on God's attributes. Herman Bavinck, *The Doctrine of God* (Grand Rapids: Eerdmans, 1951) is unsurpassed among the systematicians for a thorough treatment.

Carl Henry, *God, Revelation and Authority*, 6 vols. (Waco, TX: Word, 1976-1983) is too difficult for most readers, but it contains some valuable material on the doctrine of God for the discerning, especially in Volumes 2, 5, and 6.

The best twentieth-century works on God's attributes are A. W. Tozer, *The Knowledge of the Holy* (New York: Harper & Brothers, 1961); Arthur W. Pink, *The Attributes of God* (Swengel, PA: Reiner, 1968); J. I. Packer, *Knowing God* (Downers Grove, IL: InterVarsity, 1973); C. Samuel Storms, *The Grandeur of God: A Theological and Devotional Study of the Divine Attributes* (Grand Rapids: Baker, 1984). Tozer is the most inspiring; Pink, the most experimental; Packer, the most practical; Storms, the most theological.

If you have never read a book (other than the Bible) about God and His attributes, begin with Packer's. It's already a classic. Part 1 deals with the blessings and benefits of knowing God; Part 2 with who God is in His attributes; Part 3 with the effect God's being and attributes should have on our lives.

ARTICLE 2

By What Means God is Made Known Unto Us

John Calvin's *Institutes of the Christian Religion* (Vols. 20-21 of Library of Christian Classics; edited by John T. McNeill; translated by Ford Lewis Battles; Philadelphia: Westminster Press, 1960) is the all-time classic on the Reformed doctrine of the knowledge of God. The entire structure of *Institutes* is organized around how God is to be known as Father, Son, and Spirit. The best secondary source for Calvin's view of the knowledge of God is B. B. Warfield, "Calvin's Doctrine of the Knowledge of God," in *Calvin and Augustine* (edited by Samuel Craig; reprint Philadelphia: Presbyterian and Reformed, 1956). E. A. Dowey, Jr., *The Knowledge of God in Calvin's Theology* (1952; reprint New York: Columbia University Press, 1965), and T. H. L. Parker, *The Doctrine of the Knowledge of God: A Study in the Theology of John Calvin* (Edinburgh: Oliver and Boyd, 1952) are tinged with neo-orthodoxy. Serious students could also consult the unpublished dissertation of Kenneth Kantzer, "The Knowledge of God and the Word of God in John Calvin" (Harvard, 1950).

Additional, older works on divine revelation that are still helpful include John Brown, *A Compendious View of Natural and Revealed Religion* (Philadelphia: David Hogan, 1819), Books 1 and 2; Thomas Halyburton, "A Treatise on Natural and Revealed Religion," *The Works of the Rev. Thomas Halyburton* (London: Thomas & Tegg, 1835), pp. 254-503; George P. Fisher, *The Nature and Method of Revelation* (New York: Charles Scribner's Sons, 1890).

For twentieth-century works on the doctrine of revelation, Leon Morris's *I Believe in Revelation* (Grand Rapids: Eerdmans, 1976) is the best introductory review. Arthur W. Pink's *The Doctrine of Revelation* (Grand Rapids: Baker, 1975) focuses on God's revelation of Himself in creation, the moral nature of man, history, the Incarnation, and the Scriptures. This is the most edifying work on revelation from a popular, experimental, Reformed perspective. *The Bible: The Living Word of Revelation,* edited by Merrill Chapin Tenney (Grand Rapids: Zondervan, 1968), consists of ten essays by Evangelical Theological Society members, the bulk of which stress aspects of the doctrine of revelation, the mode of divine communication, or ramifications of inerrancy.

For in-depth Reformed works on the doctrine of revelation, consult Benjamin B. Warfield, *Revelation and Inspiration* (New York: Oxford, 1927); William Masselink, *General Revelation and Common Grace* (Grand Rapids: Eerdmans, 1953); Herman Bavinck, *The Philosophy of Revelation* (Grand Rapids: Baker, 1959); Gordon H. Clark, *Religion, Reason and Revelation* (Nutley, NJ: Presbyterian and Reformed, 1961); Cornelius VanTil, *An Introduction to Systematic Theology: Defense of the Faith* (Nutley, NJ: Presbyterian and Reformed, 1974); John H. Frame, *The Doctrine of the Knowledge of God* (Phillipsburg, NJ: Presbyterian and Reformed, 1987). G. C. Berkouwer interacts with Dutch Reformed theologians in his thought-provoking *General Revelation* (Grand Rapids: Eerdmans, 1955). Especially enlightening are Chapters 7 and 10, the latter titled, "The Controversy Regarding Article II of the Belgic Confession." As usual, however, Berkouwer asks more questions than he answers.

The most valuable study in the historical development of the doctrine of revelation is Bruce A. DeMarest, *General Revelation: Historical Views and Contemporary Issues* (Grand Rapids: Zondervan, 1982). For the post-Reformation era, see Richard Muller, *Post-Reformation Reformed Dogmatics,* Chapter 5 of Volume 1 (Grand Rapids: Baker, 1987). Also quite helpful, more detailed, and extending treatment up to 1960, is H. D. McDonald, *Theories of Revelation: An Historical Study 1700-1960* (2 vols. in 1; reprint Grand Rapids: Baker, 1979 — formerly published as *Ideas of Revelation, An Historical Study, A.D. 1700 to A.D. 1860,* and *Theories of Revelation, An Historical Study, 1860-1960).* For twentieth-century views on revelation, John Baillie, *The Idea of Revelation in Recent Thought* (New York: Columbia University Press, 1956), though often cited, is too liberal to be of much help. Of more value, though somewhat dated, is a work edited by Carl Henry, *Revelation and the Bible: Contemporary Evangelical Thought* (Grand Rapids: Baker, 1958).

Where should you start reading? Begin with Psalm 19 and Romans 1. Search the Scriptures and nature, in which God has richly revealed Himself. Peruse Calvin, Morris, Pink, and DeMarest.

ARTICLE 3

The Inspiration of the Scriptures

Articles 3-7 of the Belgic Confession address the doctrine of God's special revelation deposited in the Holy Scriptures. Concerning this doctrine, Solomon's admonition is timely: "Of making many books there is no end." The last two decades in particular have produced an endless stream of tomes at all levels about the written Word of God. For our purposes, we wish to highlight some of the best works, past and present, under the following divisions: the inspiration of the Scriptures (Article 3), the canonicity of the Scriptures (Article 4), the authority of the Scriptures (Article 5), the inferiority of the Apocrypha compared to the Scriptures (Article 6), and the sufficiency and inerrancy of the Scriptures (Article 7).

Nineteenth-century works on the Bible's divine inspiration include Robert Haldane, *The Books of the Old and New Testaments Proved to be Canonical and Their Verbal Inspiration Maintained and Established* (Boston: American Doctrinal Tract Society, 1835); Archibald Alexander, *Evidences of the Authenticity, Inspiration and Canonical Authority of the Holy Scriptures* (Philadelphia: Presbyterian Board of Publications, 1836); Louis Gaussen, *Theopneustia: The Plenary Inspiration of the Holy Scriptures* (1840; reprint Grand Rapids: Kregel, 1971); James Bannerman, *Inspiration: The Infallible Truth and Divine Authority of the Holy Scriptures* (Edinburgh: T. & T. Clark, 1865). Haldane reacts to German rationalism with verbal inspiration; Alexander's work presents numerous "evidences" but lacks his customary depth of thought; Gaussen's treatise is the nineteenth-century classic; Bannerman excels on the history of the doctrine of inspiration.

The twentieth-century classic is B. B. Warfield, *The Inspiration and Authority of the Bible*, edited by Samuel G. Craig (Philadelphia: Presbyterian and Reformed, 1970), which contains the bulk of articles (many of which have never been surpassed exegetically or theologically) in *Revelation and Inspiration* (New York: Oxford, 1927), as well as a superior 65-page introduction by Cornelius Van Til. Warfield is essential reading for understanding the "old Princeton" position on divine inspiration.

Edward J. Young, *Thy Word is Truth* (Grand Rapids: Eerdmans, 1957) does a marvelous job of combining doctrinal accuracy with popular readability. He also effectively addresses inerrancy, individual "problem texts," and modern views of Scripture.

Other helpful volumes on the popular level include: Theodore Engelder, *Scripture Cannot Be Broken* (St. Louis: Concordia, 1945), a vigorous defense of verbal-plenary inspiration; A. W. Pink, *The Divine Inspiration of the Bible* (Swengel, PA: Reiner, 1971), which aims for personal edification more than doctrinal depth; Brian Edwards, *Nothing but the Truth* (Welwyn, England: Evangelical Press, 1978), which excels for those unfamiliar with doctrinal terms and recent debate; James I. Packer, *God Has Spoken* (Downers Grove, IL: InterVarsity Press, 1979), which stresses the joy of Bible study and examines what Scripture says about itself. Packer's work includes the 1978 *Chicago Statement on Biblical Inerrancy*.

Robert Preus, *The Inspiration of Scripture*, 2nd edition (Edinburgh: Oliver and Boyd, 1957) is an able monograph on the theology of seventeenth-century Lutheran dogmaticians. For an in-depth seventeenth-century Reformed dogmatician on inspiration, see Francis Turretin, *The Doctrine of Scripture*, edited and translated by John W. Beardslee III (Grand Rapids: Baker, 1981).

Where should you begin reading? Study 2 Timothy 3:16 and 2 Peter 1:21 with the assistance of reputable commentaries. Then read Young and Edwards.

ARTICLE 4
The Canon of the Scriptures

The beginning reader should consult William J. McRae, *The Birth of the Bible* (Scarborough: Everyday Publications, 1984) or Neil Lightfoot, *How We Got Our Bible* (Grand Rapids: Baker, 1963) for a simple treatment of the establishment of the sacred canon of Scripture. On a somewhat higher level, R. Laird Harris, *Inspiration and Canonicity of the Bible* (Grand Rapids: Zondervan, 1957) is a basic, reliable work on canonization that covers most major issues. Harris lucidly argues that inspiration is the core principle of canonicity. Also, Roland K. Harrison, "The Canon of the Old Testament" and Everett F. Harrison, "The Canon of the New Testament"— articles found in most modern editions of *Young's Analytical Concordance* — are clear, concise, and sound. For a more scholarly approach to canonization, a diligent reading of William Cunningham's essay on canonicity in his *Theological Lectures* (London: Nisbet, 1878), as well as William Henry Green, *General Introduction to the Old Testament: The Canon* (London: John Murray, 1899) will reap rewards, notwithstanding their datedness. For a more recent scholarly work, consult Bruce Metzger, *The Canon of the New Testament* (Oxford: University Press, 1987).

Numerous works of "Biblical introduction" survey the Old and New Testament canon and text, covering each book's author, date and setting, theme and purpose, survey and outline. Most helpful at a simple level are William Hendriksen, *Survey of the Bible* (reprint Grand Rapids: Baker, 1976), which is reliable and short; William Deal, *Pictorial Introduction to the Bible* (Grand Rapids: Baker, 1982), which excels in practical lessons to be gleaned from each Bible book. For an intermediate level, consult John Raven, *Old Testament Introduction* (New York: Revell, 1910), which has been a conservative, somewhat dry, standard text for half a century;

Edward J. Young, *An Introduction to the Old Testament* (Grand Rapids: Eerdmans, 1960) usurps Raven as the most reliable guide to treat the major critical problems; Gleason Archer, *A Survey of Old Testament Introduction* (Chicago: Moody, 1964) ably defends the conservative evangelical position; Lawrence O. Richards, *Teacher's Commentary* (Wheaton: Victor Books, 1987) is weak on theology but excels as a practical guide for Sunday school teachers, Christian educators, and leaders of Bible-group studies. For a scholarly level, see the generally reliable works of Theodor Zahn, *Introduction to the New Testament*, 3 volumes (1909; reprint Grand Rapids: Kregel, 1953); Roland K. Harrison, *Introduction to the Old Testament* (Grand Rapids: Eerdmans, 1969); Everett F. Harrison, *Introduction to the New Testament* (Grand Rapids: Eerdmans, 1971); Donald Guthrie, *New Testament Introduction*, 4th revised edition (Downers Grove, IL: InterVarsity, 1990); D. A. Carson, Douglas J. Moo, and Leon Morris, *An Introduction to the New Testament* (Grand Rapids: Zondervan, 1992); Raymond B. Dillard and Tremper Logman III, *An Introduction to the Old Testament* (Grand Rapids: Zondervan, 1995).

Begin with R. Laird Harris.

ARTICLE 5

The Authority of Scripture

The two most helpful books on biblical authority are *The Infallible Word: A Symposium by the Members of the Faculty of Westminster Theological Seminary*, edited by Ned Stonehouse and Paul Woolley (Philadelphia: Presbyterian and Reformed, 1946) and Bernard Ramm, *The Pattern of Religious Authority* (Grand Rapids: Eerdmans, 1957). The symposium contains an excellent series of Reformed essays dealing with the general character of biblical authority and canonicity. It concludes by stressing the relevancy and distinctive characteristics of these doctrines as well as the importance of preaching them.

Ramm addresses issues on authority that confront the conservative evangelical. He distinguishes between the "grounds of accepting an authority" and "the right of authority," and claims that reason, intuition, or inclination are modes of perceiving or receiving an authority but do not constitute the right of the authority received. He argues that the believer's doctrine of authority is threefold: the authority of the Scriptures, of the Holy Spirit, and of Christ. This threefold delineation is contrasted with Roman Catholicism, modernism, and neo-orthodoxy.

Helpful articles by John Gerstner, James Packer, Francis Schaeffer, R. C. Sproul, and others can be found in *The Foundation of Biblical Authority*, edited by James M. Boice (Grand Rapids: Zondervan, 1978), which is the first major publication of the International Council on Biblical Inerrancy (ICBI), founded in 1977. Volume 4 of Carl Henry, *God, Revelation and Authority* (Waco, TX: Word, 1979) contains a massive technical treatment of biblical authority. Meredith Kline, *The Structure of Biblical Authority* (Grand Rapids: Eerdmans, 1972) argues that our understanding of authority can be forwarded by relating the concept of canon to the treaty documents of the ancient Near East. John D. Woodbridge, *Biblical Authority: A Critique of the Rogers/McKim Proposal* (Grand Rapids: Zondervan, 1982) effectively exposes the sloppy scholarship of Rogers and McKim, and it positively addresses the issue of biblical authority for our day from a conservative, evangelical perspective.

For historical studies on biblical authority, consult Rupert Eric Davies, *The Problem of Authority in the Continental Reformers: A Study in Luther, Zwingli, and Calvin* (London: Epworth Press, 1946); Henry Jackson Forstman, *Calvin's Doctrine of Biblical Authority* (Stanford: Stanford University Press, 1962), which includes a helpful epilogue on "Calvin, Calvinism, and the Contemporary Situation" as well as an excellent bibliography.

Where should you begin? Read a persuasive, little book by D. Martyn Lloyd-Jones titled *Authority* (London: Inter-Varsity, 1966), which is a clarion call to return to the authority of Christ, the Word, and the Holy Spirit.

ARTICLE 6
The Apocrypha

Sources for the Apocrypha include:

(1) *King James Version*: Most KJV pulpit Bibles include the Apocrypha, as does Thomas Nelson's 1990 reprint of the 1611 KJV.

(2) *Geneva Bible*: See the 1969 facsimile of the 1560 edition published by the University of Wisconsin Press.

(3) *Reims-Douay*: The apocryphal books are interspersed with the canonical books in keeping with the Roman Catholic tradition.

(4) *Revised Version*: The Apocrypha was published in 1894 as a sequel to the RV of 1881 (see *The World's Classic Series*, vol. 294 [Oxford University Press]).

(5) *Revised Standard Version*: "The Oxford Annotated Apocrypha," edited by Bruce Metzger (New York: Oxford, 1965; also printed as part of *The New Oxford Annotated Bible with the Apocrypha* [1973]), is a very helpful edition.

The Apocrypha and Pseudepigrapha, edited by Robert H. Charles in two volumes with introductions and explanatory notes (Oxford: 1913, reprint: Clarendon Press, 1963), is the standard critical work. William Oesterley, *An Introduction to the Books of the Apocrypha* (London: SPCK, 1946) has been superseded by Bruce M. Metzger, *An Introduction to the Apocrypha* (New York: Oxford, 1957). Metzger provides a comprehensive examination of the books of the Apocrypha, together with an evaluation of their history and significance. David Russell, *Between the Testaments* (London: SCM Press, 1960) and Herbert Andrews, *An Introduction to the Apocryphal Books of the Old and New Testament*, revised and edited by Charles F. Pfeiffer (Grand Rapids: Baker, 1964) address the cultural and literary background of the Apocrypha. Roland K. Harrison,

Introduction to the Old Testament (Grand Rapids: Eerdmans, 1969) provides a special, 100-page supplement on the Apocrypha.

Where should you begin? Read the Apocrypha and E. J. Goodspeed, *The Story of the Apocrypha* (Chicago, 1939), followed by Harrison and Metzger's *Introduction*.

ARTICLE 7
Scripture's Sufficiency and Inerrancy

Sufficiency

Numerous books touch on the sufficiency of Scripture, but none addresses both the long-standing and contemporary issues involved in such an able, engaging, and readable manner as Noel Weeks, *The Sufficiency of Scripture* (Edinburgh: Banner of Truth Trust, 1988). The first part deals with basic issues such as authority, revelation, providence, inerrancy, and contextualization; the remainder of the volume addresses specific points of contention, such as creation, the interpretation of prophecy, women in church offices, psychology, and Bible translation.

James I. Packer, *Beyond the Battle for the Bible* (Westchester, IL: Cornerstone, 1980) deals with the sufficiency of Scripture in a lengthy chapter on how to use Scripture in public and private. It also addresses the current debate on inerrancy.

Inerrancy

A helpful, readable book that defends inerrancy on the basis of Christ's view of Scripture is Robert P. Lightner, *The Saviour and the Scriptures* (Philadelphia: Presbyterian and Reformed, 1966). *God's Inerrant Word*, edited by John W. Montgomery (Minneapolis: Bethany, 1974), is a collection of superior essays written prior to Lindsell's books.

Harold Lindsell, *The Battle for the Bible* (Grand Rapids: Zondervan, 1976) gave the inerrancy debate fresh impetus by documenting evidence of substantial erosion of commitment to this doctrine in evangelical denominations and schools. In a sequel volume, *The Bible in the Balance* (Grand Rapids: Zondervan, 1979),

Lindsell fleshes out his arguments, answers his critics, and cites further inerrancy erosion in churches and schools.

Some of the best material on the Reformed view of inerrancy can be found in several collections of essays published in the 1980s, including *Inerrancy and Common Sense*, edited by Roger R. Nicole and J. Ramsey Michaels (Grand Rapids: Baker, 1980); *Inerrancy*, edited by Norman L. Geisler (Grand Rapids: Zondervan, 1980); *Scripture and Truth*, edited by D. A. Carson and John D. Woodbridge (Grand Rapids: Zondervan, 1983); *Inerrancy and the Church*, edited by John D. Hannah (Chicago: Moody Press, 1984); *Challenges to Inerrancy: A Theological Response*, edited by Gordon R. Lewis and Bruce Demarest (Chicago: Moody Press, 1984); *Hermeneutics, Inerrancy, and the Bible*, edited by Earl D. Radmacher and Robert D. Preus (Grand Rapids: Zondervan, 1984); *Evangelicals and Inerrancy*, edited by Ronald Youngblood (New York: Thomas Nelson, 1984); *Inerrancy and Hermeneutics*, edited by Harvie Conn (Grand Rapids: Baker, 1988).

A word of warning: Avoid G. C. Berkouwer, *Holy Scripture*, translated by Jack Rogers (Grand Rapids: Eerdmans, 1975). Berkouwer qualifies inerrancy by disassociating it from historical and scientific exactness. He neglects to spell out the dangerous consequences of tolerating arbitrary rejection of selected Scriptures.

Where should you begin reading on inerrancy? For a brief, nontechnical starter, read John H. Gerstner, *Bible Inerrancy Primer* (Grand Rapids: Baker, 1965).

ARTICLES 8-9

The Trinity

During the earliest centuries of church history, the Christian doctrine of God as "three persons in one substance or essence" assumed the shape that has been largely retained ever since. Athanasius and the Cappadocians in the fourth century, and later, Augustine, played a critical role. The Apostles', the Nicene, and the Athanasian creeds embody the core teachings of the fathers on the Trinity. For primary sources on the development of Trinitarian doctrine in the ancient church, see *Ante-Nicene Fathers*, edited by Alexander Robert and James Donaldson, 10 volumes (1885-96; reprint Grand Rapids: Eerdmans, 1951-56), and *Nicene and Post-Nicene Fathers*, edited by Philip Schaff et al., two series of 14 volumes each (1887-94; reprint Grand Rapids: Eerdmans, 1952-56). For secondary studies, see W. S. Bishop, *The Development of Trinitarian doctrine in the Nicene and Athanasian Creeds* (New York: Longmans, Green, 1910); L. Prestige, *God in Patristic Thought*, 2nd ed. (London: SPCK, 1952); J. Quasten, *Patrology*, 3 vols. (1950-86; reprint Westminster, MD: Christian Classics, 1983-86); J. N. D. Kelly, *The Athanasian Creed* (London: A. & C. Black, 1964), *Early Christian Doctrines* (New York: Harper & Row, 1965), and *Early Christian Creeds* (London: Longmans, 1972); Edmund J. Fortman, *The Triune God: A Historical Study of the Doctrine of the Trinity* (Philadelphia: Westminster, 1972); and Thomas F. Torrance, *The Trinitarian Faith: The Evangelical Theology of the Ancient Catholic Church* (Edinburgh: T. and T. Clark, 1988).

Surprisingly, few helpful books are written on the Trinity from a sound Reformed perspective, considering that the Reformers were very concerned to affirm their unity with the ancient church in this doctrine. Standard Reformed dogmatics often have valuable sections on the Trinity; consult especially Calvin's *Institutes*, which is organized around a Trinitarian framework. The best Puritan works on the Trinity are Volume 2 of John Owen's *Works* (reprint Edinburgh: Banner of Truth Trust, 1965) and the last one hundred pages of Volume 2 of John Howe's *Works* (reprint Ligonier, PA: Soli Deo Gloria, 1990). Owen's major work in Volume 2, *Of Communion with God the Father, Son, and Holy Ghost* (365 pages), is unsurpassed in Christian literature in detailing how the believer experimentally communes with each person in the Trinity. Also, consult B. B. Warfield, "The Biblical Doctrine of the Trinity," in *Biblical and Theological Studies*, edited by Samuel G. Craig (Philadelphia: Presbyterian and Reformed, 1968), pp. 22-59.

There are four, recommendable, popular-level works on the Trinity. A nineteenth-century classic, Edward H. Bickersteth, *The Trinity* (reprint Grand Rapids: Kregel, 1965) is the best older work. First published in 1859 under the title, *The Rock of Ages*, this little work promotes a worshipful tone in approaching the doctrine of the Trinity and provides considerable biblical evidence for belief in the eternal Godhead of the Father, Son, and Spirit. The concluding chapter, "Faith, the Scriptures, and the Trinity," is particularly helpful. Also reliable and basic is Loraine Boettner's section on the Trinity in *Studies in Theology* (1947; reprint Grand Rapids: Baker, 1975), pp. 79-138. The most readable, contemporary works on the Trinity are Stuart Olyott, *The Three are One* (Welwyn, Herts: Evangelical Press, 1979), and Alister E. McGrath, *Understanding the Trinity* (Grand Rapids: Zondervan, 1990).

For works of greater depth, consult the following: G. A. F. Knight, *A Biblical Approach to the Doctrine of the Trinity* (Edinburgh: Oliver and Boyd, 1953) and E. Calvin Beisner, *God in Three Persons* (Wheaton: Tyndale, 1984) provide an account of the biblical foundations of the doctrine of the Trinity. A. W. Wainwright, *The Trinity in the New Testament* (London: SPCK, 1962) argues that the doctrine of the Trinity is essential to the New Testament message. *One God in Trinity* (Westchester, IL: Cornerstone, 1980), edited by Peter Toon and James D. Spiceland, contains lectures of varying merit delivered at the British Tyndale Fellowship, Durham, 1978. Gordon H. Clark, *The Trinity* (Jefferson, MD: Trinity Foundation, 1985) is a clear historical-theological work on the church's understanding of the doctrine of the Trinity during the past two millenia. This book suffers, however, from being overly critical of

Bavinck, VanTil, Knudsen, and others. Royce Gordon Gruenler, *The Trinity in the Gospel of John* (Grand Rapids: Baker, 1986) is a careful study of the Trinity as presented in John's gospel. Millard J. Erickson, *God in Three Persons: A Contemporary Interpretation of the Trinity* (Grand Rapids: Baker, 1995) is the latest and best all-around work on the Trinity. It covers the Trinity in the Old Testament, the New Testament, and early church history, as well as defends the ongoing importance of a Trinitarian definition of God. Erickson also effectively addresses contemporary questions about the Trinity. This volume, geared to undergraduate theological courses, will no doubt become a staple work, but there remains a need for a biblical, historical, and theological work on the Trinity from a thoroughly Reformed perspective.

For a starter, try Bickersteth. Move on to Calvin, but do not rest until you digest the sublime, second volume of Owen's *Works*.

ARTICLE 10
The Deity of Jesus Christ

The best seventeenth-century works on Christ's deity and glory are from the prince of Puritans, John Owen (1616-1683). Three moving treatises are collected in Volume 1 of the Goold edition of Owen's *Works*, reprinted by Banner of Truth Trust in 1965 and several times thereafter: *A Declaration of the Glorious Mystery of the Person of Christ* (1679), *Meditations and Discourses on the Glory of Christ* (1684), and *Meditations and Discourses Concerning the Glory of Christ Applied* (1691). With regard to the glory of Christ's divine person, Owen's treatises remain unsurpassed. Thomas M'Crie writes of Owen's works on Christ in Volume 1, "Of all the theological works published by individuals since the Reformation, next to Calvin's *Institutes*, we should have deemed it our highest honour to have produced [these]."

Helpful eighteenth-century works on the Godhead of the Son include August Hermann Francke, *Christus Sacrae Scripturae Nucleus: Or, Christ The Sum and Substance Of all the Holy Scriptures* (London: J. Downing, 1732), which focuses on the divinity of Christ in John 1 in a judicious and heart-warming manner; John Guyse, *Jesus Christ God-Man: or, The Constitution of Christ's Person, with the Evidence and Importance of the Doctrine of His True and Proper Godhead* (Glasgow: David Niven, 1790), which is a series of sermons expounding Romans 9:5; William Laing, *Philemon's Letters to Onesimus: Upon The Subjects of Christ's Atonement and Divinity* (Newry: D. Carpenter, 1791), which is an able, 432-page defense of Christ's divinity in sixteen engaging letters; Robert Hawker, *Sermons on the Divinity of Christ* (1792; reprint London: E. Spettigue, 1847), which includes eight moving sermons by an experiential, Calvinist Anglican that spell out the spiritual and daily ramifications of believing in Christ as the Son of God.

Noteworthy nineteenth-century works on Christ's deity include Ambrose Serle, *Horae Solitariae: Or, Essays Upon some Remarkable Names and Titles of Jesus Christ, Occurring in the Old Testament, and Declarative of His Essential Divinity...*, Volume 1 (Dublin: Thomas Connolly, 1849), which is particularly helpful in proving Christ's divinity from the Old Testament; Henry Parry Liddon, *The Divinity of Our Lord and Saviour Jesus Christ* (1868; reprint Minneapolis: Klock & Klock, 1978), which is a standard, frequently reprinted treatment of Liddon's Bampton lectures; Joseph C. Philpot, *Eternal Sonship of Christ* (1865; reprint Grand Rapids: Sovereign Grace, 1971), which is a scriptural, polemical, and experiential treatment.

Several twentieth-century books uphold an orthodox view of Christ's divinity in an edifying manner. Benjamin B. Warfield, *The Lord of Glory* (London: Hodder and Stoughton, 1907) provides a scholarly examination of the biblical evidence for the deity of Christ. Robert Anderson, *The Lord from Heaven* (1910; reprint Grand Rapids: Kregel, 1978) ably expounds Christ's deity from both testaments, focusing on Him as King of kings. William E. Vine, *The Divine Sonship of Christ*, 2 vols. in 1 (Minneapolis: Klock & Klock, 1984) contains *Christ's Eternal Sonship* and *The First and the Last*, both of which emphasize the benefits that flow to the believer from Christ's divinity. Herbert Lockyer, *All the Divine Names and Titles in the Bible* (Grand Rapids: Zondervan, 1975) devotes two hundred pages to an edifying exposition of scores of Christ's names that shed light on His divinity. Josh McDowell and Bart Larson, *Jesus: A Biblical Defense of His Deity* (San Bernardino, CA: Here's Life, 1983) is designed as an apologetic for college students. Murray J. Harris, *Jesus as God: The New Testament Use of Theos in Reference to God* (Grand Rapids: Baker, 1992) carefully exegetes ten texts in an evangelical, scholarly manner and provides an excellent up-to-date bibliography.

For the historical development of the doctrine of Christ's divinity, see Edward Burton, *Testimonies of Ante-Nicene Fathers to the Divinity of Christ*, 2nd ed. (Oxford, 1829); Izaak August Dorner, *History of the Development of the Doctrine of the Person of Christ*, 5 vols. (Edinburgh, 1861-63); Albert Reville, *History of the Doctrine of the Deity of Jesus Christ* (London, 1870).

Where should you begin? Read the gospel of John again, paying particular regard to the apostle's affirmations of Christ's divinity (see also A. T. Robertson, *The Divinity of Christ in the Gospel of John* [1916; reprint Grand Rapids: Baker, 1976]). Then read some of the creedal statements of the ancient church, such as the Nicene, Chalcedonian, and Athanasian creeds. Follow this up with a reading of John H. Gerstner's helpful, introductory booklet, *A Primer on the Deity of Christ* (Phillipsburg, NJ: Presbyterian and Reformed, 1984).

ARTICLE 11

The Deity of the Holy Spirit

Some scholars say that the Holy Spirit is the forgotten person of the Trinity, but Reformed theologians have produced numerous tomes on the work of the Spirit, including several classics written by such capable Puritans as John Owen and Thomas Goodwin. Much less, however, has been written on the Person of the Spirit, particularly on His deity. Frequently books on the Holy Spirit include a short chapter on the divinity of the Spirit but do not address this important subject in depth. Even John Owen's third chapter in *A Discourse Concerning the Holy Spirit*, titled, "Divine Nature and Personality of the Holy Spirit Proved and Vindicated" (*Works*, Volume 3, reprint Banner of Truth Trust, 1965), while supplying a solid foundation and polemical defense (especially against the Socinians) for the Spirit's deity, lacks the author's characteristic thoroughness. A definitive work on the Spirit's divinity, together with its implications, has yet to be written from a biblical, Reformed perspective.

The most helpful eighteenth-century works devoted to expounding the Godhead of the Spirit include John Guyse, *The Holy Spirit a Divine Person: or, the Doctrine of His Godhead represented as evident and important* (Glasgow: David Niven, 1790), which includes a series of sermons expounding 1 Corinthians 12:11; Robert Hawker, *Sermons on the Deity and Operations of the Holy Spirit* (1792; reprint London: E. Spettigue, 1847), which includes eight sermons that spell out the spiritual and daily ramifications of believing in the Spirit as the third person of the Trinity.

Noteworthy nineteenth-century volumes that address the Spirit's deity include Ambrose Serle, *Horae Solitariae: Or, Essays Upon some Names, Titles, and Attributes of the Holy Spirit, revealed in the Two Testaments...*, Volume 2 (Dublin: Thomas Connolly, 1849), which is a fascinating, 450-page work expounding twenty-eight names and attributes ascribed to the Spirit in the Scriptures, conclusively proving His divinity and bringing that divinity to bear upon daily, Christian living. Edward Bickersteth, *The Spirit of Life* (1850; reprinted as *The Holy Spirit: His Person and Work* [Grand Rapids: Kregel, 1959]) provides a readable, scriptural summary of the eternalness of the Spirit's Godhead. Robert Balmer, "On the Divinity of the Holy Spirit," in *Theological Tracts, Selected and Original*, edited by John Brown (London: A. Fullarton, 1854), pp. 186-203, is a helpful, succinct treatment. Joseph C. Philpot, *Meditations on the Person, Work and Covenant Offices of God the Holy Ghost* (1865; reprint Harpenden, Herts: O. G. Pearce, 1976) devotes three chapters to aspects of the Spirit's deity in a helpful, scriptural, and experiential manner. George Smeaton, *The Doctrine of the Holy Spirit* (1882; reprint Edinburgh: Banner of Truth Trust, 1958) combines theological accuracy with practical teaching in expounding the Spirit's deity in relation to the doctrine of the Trinity.

Several twentieth-century books uphold an orthodox view of the Spirit's divinity but add little to the older works. The first four chapters of R. C. Sproul, *The Mystery of the Holy Spirit* (Wheaton: Tyndale, 1990) is helpful for anyone struggling with the deity of the Spirit and the mystery of the Trinity.

For a listing of more than 2,000 works written on various aspects of the person and work of the Holy Spirit, see Watson E. Mills, *The Holy Spirit: A Bibliography* (Peabody, MA: Hendrickson, 1988).

Begin with George Smeaton. His work on the Spirit is readable, thorough, and edifying.

ARTICLE 12

Creation, Angels, and Devils

Creation

A plethora of books and articles have been written in recent decades on creation and/or science. The best series of articles on creation from a Reformed perspective is "Symposium on Creation," in *The Journal of Christian Reconstruction* 1 (Summer 1974). For an in-depth study of Genesis 1, especially the first three verses and their interrelationship, see Edward J. Young, *Studies in Genesis One* (Philadelphia: Presbyterian and Reformed, 1973; originally published in the *Westminster Theological Journal* as three articles).

Helpful books include Rousas J. Rushdoony, *Mythology of Science* (Nutley, NJ: Craig, 1967), which exposes a number of naive theories long held by secular scientists; Walter E. Lammerts, ed., *Scientific Studies in Special Creation* (Grand Rapids: Baker, 1971), which effectively answers basic questions about special creation; and R. L. Wysong, *The Creation-Evolution Controversy* (East Lansing, MI: Inquiry, 1976), which fully supports Scripture's account of creation on revelatory and reasoned grounds.

For additional books advocating biblical creationism, contact the Institute for Creation Research (ICR), in San Diego, California. Consult the writings of institute scientist Duane T. Gish (such as *Up With Creation* [San Diego: Creation-Life, 1974] and *The Battle for Creation* [San Diego: Creation-Life, 1976]), and especially those of the institute's president, Henry M. Morris (e.g., *Evolution in Turmoil* [San Diego: Creation-Life, 1982]; *The Biblical Basis for Modern Science* [Grand Rapids: Baker, 1984]; *A History of Modern Creationism* [San Diego: Master, 1984]; *The Long War Against God: The History and Impact of the Creation/Evolution Conflict* [Grand Rapids: Baker, 1989]).

Angels

An old, scarce, but valuable work that focuses on the ministry of angels to believers is "The Ministration of, and Communion with Angels," in *The Works of Isaac Ambrose* (London: Tegg, 1810), pp. 473-560. Ambrose (1604-1663) was one of the most meditative of Puritans; he annually took the month of May for solitary retreat. His *magnum opus* is the classic *Looking Unto Jesus* (1658).

Alexander Whyte, *The Nature of Angels* (1930; reprint Grand Rapids: Baker, 1976), though a bit imaginative at times, remains a helpful book of eight, expository sermons addressing different aspects of angelology.

For shorter but enlightening pieces on the biblical doctrine of the angels, see "On the Ministry of Angels," in *The Works of John Newton* (reprint Edinburgh: Nelson, 1839), letter #41, pp. 123-126; Henry Harbaugh, "Angelic Sympathy," in *Heaven* (Philadelphia: Lindsay and Blakiston, 1854), pp. 221-257; *The Works of Jonathan Edwards*, Vol. 2 (1834; reprint Edinburgh: Banner of Truth Trust, 1974), pp. 141-156, 604-617. For Edwards's views on angels, see John H. Gerstner, *The Rational Theology of Jonathan Edwards* (Powhatan, VA: Berea, 1992), 2:203-236.

For a historical-theological approach, consult E. Langton, *The Ministries of the Angelic Powers According to the Old Testament and Later Jewish Literature* (London: Clarke, 1936); G. B. Caird, *Principalities and Powers: A Study in Pauline Theology* (Oxford: Clarendon, 1956); J. Danielou, *The Angels and their Mission According to the Fathers of the Church*, translated by D. Heimann (Westminster: Newman, 1957); G. Davidson, *A Dictionary of Angels* (New York: Free Press, 1967).

Devils

The best over-all contemporary study of biblical demonology is Frederick S. Leahy, *Satan Cast Out* (Edinburgh: Banner of Truth Trust, 1975). For books on combating Satan's temptations, two classics still stand head-and-shoulders above the rest: Thomas Brooks, *Precious Remedies Against Satan's Devices* (London: Baynes, 1804), which is presently available in Banner of Truth Trust's Puritan paperback reprint series; and Richard Gilpin, *Daemonologia Sacra; or, A Treatise of Satan's Temptations* (Edinburgh: James Nichol, 1867).

Other good titles include A. W. Pink, *Satan and His Gospel* (Swengel, PA: Reiner, n.d.); Edward M. Bounds, *Satan: His*

Personality, Power and Overthrow (reprint Grand Rapids: Baker, 1972); C. S. Lewis, *Screwtape Letters* (reprint New York: Macmillan, 1969).

For more scholarly works, consult E. Langton, *Satan, A Portrait: A Study of the Character of Satan Through All the Ages* (London: Skeffington, 1945) and *Essentials of Demonology: A Study of Jewish and Christian Doctrine* (London: Epworth, 1949); S. Eitrem, *Some Notes on the Demonology in the New Testament* (Oslo: Universitetsforlager, 1966); J. B. Russell, *Satan: The Early Christian Tradition* (Ithaca: Cornell, 1981); E. Ferguson, *Demonology of the Early Christian World* (New York: Mellen, 1984).

Where should you turn for a Reformed exposition on the creation of the world and the angels, as well as the reality of devils? Try Benjamin B. Warfield's excellent essay, "Calvin's Doctrine of the Creation" in *Calvin and Calvinism* (New York: Oxford, 1931), pp. 287-351, which addresses Calvin's view of the angels and devils as well as of creation as a whole.

ARTICLE 13

Divine Providence

The best work by a church father on the doctrine of providence is Augustine, *Divine Providence*, translated by R. P. Russell, in *The Fathers of the Church*, Volume 5 (Washington, D.C.: Catholic University of America Press, 1948). See also the writings of John Chrysostom, sometimes dubbed "the great theologian of providence" (e.g., *No One Can Harm the Man Who Does Not Injure Himself*, translated by W. R. Stephens, in *Nicene and Post-Nicene Fathers*, edited by P. Schaff, et al., Series 1, Volume 9 [reprint Grand Rapids: Eerdmans, 1954]).

For a classic, Reformed treatment of providence, consult *Calvin's Calvinism: Treatises on the Eternal Predestination of God & the Secret Providence of God*, translated by Henry Cole (reprint Grand Rapids: Reformed Free, 1991), in which Calvin defends the sovereignty of God in providence (pp. 210-350). For a broader, more concise treatment of providence by Calvin, read *Institutes of the Christian Religion*, Book 1, Chapters 16-18 (pp. 197-237 of Volume 1, edited by John T. McNeill and translated by Ford Lewis Battles [Philadelphia: Westminster Press, 1960]). For an excellent treatment of providence by Calvin's successor, Theodore Beza, try Ian McPhee, "Conserver or Transformer of Calvin's Theology? A Study of the Origins and Development of Theodore Beza's Thought, 1550-1570" (Ph.D. dissertation, Cambridge University, 1979), pp. 226-290. For additional Reformed sources on providence, consult Heinrich Heppe, *Reformed Dogmatics: Set Out and Illustrated From the Sources*, translated by G. T. Thomson (1950; reprint Grand Rapids: Baker, 1978), pp. 251-280, as well as standard systematic theologies, such as those by Louis Berkhof and Charles Hodge.

The Puritans superseded the Reformers in handling the doctrine of providence in an experiential, practical manner. The classic in the field is John Flavel, *Divine Conduct: or, The Mystery of Providence* (reprint London: Banner of Truth Trust, 1963; see also Volume 4 of Flavel's *Works*, pp. 336-497). First published in 1678 and reprinted dozens of times, this classic shows how divine providence affects every aspect of a believer's life. It is an invaluable work for instructing God's children in understanding and bowing under God's purposes for their lives. Flavel knew of what he wrote; often persecuted and narrowly escaping arrest on several occasions, his personal life was full of trials. Three times he was left a widower. He died suddenly at the age of sixty-four, confessing, "I know it shall be well with me."

Second-best among the Puritans on providence is Stephen Charnock, "A Treatise on Divine Providence" in *Complete Works*, Volume 1 (Edinburgh: James Nichol, 1864), pp. 3-120. Two excellent Puritan sermons succinctly summarizing the benefits of providence for the believer are Ezekiel Hopkins, *Works*, Volume 3 (Philadelphia: Leighton, 1867; reprint Morgan, PA: Soli Deo Gloria, 1997), pp. 368-388 (on Matthew 10:29-30); and Thomas Lye, "How Are We to Live by Faith on Divine Providence?" in *Puritan Sermons 1659-1689: Being the Morning Exercises at Cripplegate*, Volume 1 (reprint Wheaton: Richard Owen Roberts, 1981), pp. 369-400 (on Psalm 57:8).

The most readable and recommendable nineteenth-century treatment of providence is William S. Plumer, *Jehovah-jireh: A Treatise on Providence* (1865; reprint Harrisonburg, VA: Sprinkle, 1993). Separate chapters discuss God's providence as mysterious, retributive, kind, and vast. Chapter 16, "God's Providence Towards His Church Renders Unnecessary All Tormenting Fears Respecting Her Safety and Final Triumph," is particularly helpful. Hosea Preslar, *Thoughts on Divine Providence, Or a Sketch of God's Care Over and Dealings with His People* (1867; reprint Streamwood, IL: Primitive Baptist Library, 1977) is doctrinally inferior to Plumer but does afford an edifying treatment of providence from a more biographical perspective. Alexander Carson provides us with two frequently reprinted books that trace the acts of providence throughout Scripture: *The History of Providence as explained in the Bible* (reprint Grand Rapids: Baker, 1977) and *Confidence In God in Times of Danger: God's Providence Unfolded in the Book of Esther* (reprint Swengel, PA: Bible Truth Depot, 1962).

Two twentieth-century monographs on providence are noteworthy: Gerrit C. Berkouwer, *The Providence of God*, translated by Lewis B. Smedes (Grand Rapids: Eerdmans, 1952), asks thought-provoking questions about providence in relation to knowledge, sustenance, government, concurrence, history, miracles, and theodicy. Benjamin B. Farley, *The Providence of God* (Grand Rapids: Baker, 1988) is the best study of the development of the doctrine of providence throughout history from a Reformed perspective.

Where should you begin? Read Flavel, then Plumer.

ARTICLE 14

Our Creation, Fall, and Bound Will

Our Creation

The best twentieth-century works from a Reformed perspective on our creation in God's image are Gerrit C. Berkouwer, *Man: The Image of God,* translated by Dirk W. Jellema (Grand Rapids: Eerdmans, 1962); Anthony A. Hoekema, *Created in God's Image* (Grand Rapids: Eerdmans, 1986); and Philip Edgcumbe Hughes, *The True Image: The Origin and Destiny of Man in Christ* (Grand Rapids: Eerdmans, 1989). Berkouwer provides an in-depth treatment that interacts with numerous (especially Dutch) theologians; Hoekema's volume is a readable, comprehensive study of the biblical doctrine of man. It upholds the traditional Reformed balance between the image of God in a narrower or structural sense (what man is), and in a broader or functional sense (what man does). Hughes presents a wide-ranging biblical, historical, and theological study that profoundly integrates the doctrines of man and Christ.

Two excellent introductions to the Reformed doctrine of man written on a popular level are J. Gresham Machen, *The Christian View of Man* (1935; London: Banner of Truth Trust, 1965) and James I. Packer, *Knowing Man* (Westchester, IL: Cornerstone, 1979).

Other recommendable volumes include Wallie A. Criswell, *Did Man Just Happen?* (Grand Rapids: Zondervan, 1957), which deals on a popular level with the factual material relating to the creation of man, the evidence of biology for special creation, and the mystery of man; Leonard Verduin, *Somewhat Less Than God: The Biblical View of Man* (Grand Rapids: Eerdmans, 1970), which offers a systematic approach to the Christian doctrine of man; Francis Nigel Lee, *The Origin and Destiny of Man* (Nutley, NJ: Presbyterian and Reformed,

1974), which includes five biblical lectures delivered at the inauguration of the Christian Studies Center in Memphis; Paul Brand and Philip Yancey, *Fearfully and Wonderfully Made* (Grand Rapids: Zondervan, 1980), which discusses the marvels of God's handiwork in the human body; Gordon H. Clark, *The Biblical Doctrine of Man* (Jefferson, MD: Trinity Foundation, 1984), which compares Christian and humanist views of man.

For significant historical studies, see J. E. Sullivan, *The Image of God: The Doctrine of St. Augustine and Its Influence* (Dubuque: Priory, 1963); Thomas F. Torrance, *Calvin's Doctrine of Man* (London: Lutterworth Press, 1949).

Our Fall

The best devotional, expository study of Genesis 3 that provides a careful exegesis of the original text is Edward J. Young, *Genesis Three* (London: Banner of Truth Trust, 1966). No Reformed theologian, however, has matched Calvin's superb treatment of the fall, in the opening chapters of Book Two of his *Institutes*.

For fostering personal conviction of our tragic fall and profound sin in Adam, read Thomas Boston, *Human Nature in Its Fourfold State* (1720; London: Banner of Truth Trust, 1964). This classic focuses on our four states of innocence, depravity, grace, and glory, but Boston's section on our imputed and inherited depravity is especially poignant. He details how our sin in Adam tragically and radically broke our relationship with God, as well as each of the Ten Commandments. For a twentieth-century Boston, read Arthur W. Pink, *Gleanings from the Scriptures: Man's Total Depravity* (Chicago: Moody, 1969).

For historical studies marred by liberal thinking but providing valuable source material, consult F. R. Tennant, *The Sources of the Doctrines of the Fall and Original Sin* (Cambridge: University Press, 1903) and N. P. Williams, *The Ideas of the Fall and of Original Sin* (London: Longmans, Green, 1927).

The Bondage of Man's Will

Augustine laid the groundwork for Reformed treatises on the bondage of our will in *On the Grace of Christ* and *On Original Sin* (two treatises written in 418 A.D.), and *On Grace and Free Will* (written in 426 A.D.). They can be found in English in *Saint Augustin's Anti-Pelagian Works*, translated by Peter Holmes and Robert Wallis and revised by Benjamin B. Warfield, *Nicene and Post-Nicene Fathers*, edited by Philip Schaff (Grand Rapids: Eerdmans, 1991), First Series, Volume 5, pp. 214-257, 436-467.

Three Protestant classics have been written on the bondage of the will: Martin Luther, *The Bondage of the Will*, translated by J. I. Packer and O. R. Johnston (Westwood, NJ: Revell, 1957), is a modern, accurate translation of Luther's reply to the diatribe of Erasmus, *De Servo Arbitrio*. Erasmus realized that Luther's classic ably expounded one of the major themes of the Reformation's gospel message. (For a good translation of both documents in one volume, see *Luther and Erasmus on Free Will*, translated and edited by E. Gordon Rupp and Philip S. Watson [Philadelphia: Westminster Press, 1969].) John Calvin's less famous work on the will has finally been translated into English. It's *The Bondage and Liberation of the Will: A Defence of the Orthodox Doctrine of Human Choice against Pighius*, edited by A.N.S. Lane, translated by G.I. Davies (Grand Rapids: Baker, 1996). While Calvin's work is not as significant as Luther's, it is his fullest treatment of the relation between grace and free will, and it contains important material not found elsewhere in his writings. Jonathan Edwards, *Freedom of the Will*, edited by Paul Ramsey, Volume 1 of *The Works of Jonathan Edwards* (1754; New Haven: Yale, 1957) is a detailed inquiry into the prevailing theory of Edwards's day regarding the freedom of the will and human determinism. Edwards employed the distinction between natural and moral inability. Fallen man's inability to do good is a moral inability, consisting of the opposition or lack of inclination to good. It is not a natural inability.

For further Puritan sources, read the statement on free will in *The Westminster Confession of Faith*, Chapter 9, as well as John Owen, who effectively addresses questions that swirl around free will in *Display of Arminianism*, Volume 10 of *The Works of John Owen* (reprint London: Banner of Truth Trust, 1968), pp. 1-140.

For historical-theological studies, see William Cunningham's essay, "Calvinism, and the Doctrine of Philosophical Necessity," in *The Reformers and the Theology of the Reformation* (1862; reprint London: Banner of Truth Trust, 1967). It's an invaluable guide for understanding the view of the Reformers on the will of man. Harry J. McSorley, *Luther: Right or Wrong? An Ecumenical-Theological Study of Luther's Major Work, The Bondage of the Will* (Minneapolis: Augsburg, 1967) contains valuable, primary-source material reviewing issues involving the bondage of the will in Augustine, Thomas Aquinas, and Luther (notwithstanding the author's erroneous conclusions), as well as a superb bibliography.

For popular treatments, read *God's Will, Man's Will, and Free Will: Four Discussions by Horatius Bonar, Jonathan Edwards, Charles H. Spurgeon, and Jay Green* (Wilmington: Sovereign Grace, 1972); W. E. Best, *Free Grace Versus Free Will* (Grand Rapids: Baker, 1977); John H. Gerstner, *A Primer on Free Will* (Phillipsburg, NJ: Presbyterian and Reformed, 1982).

For additional books on creation, see bibliographical notes on Article 12, and for additional books on our fall, see notes on Article 15.

ARTICLE 15
Original Sin

Augustine's brief treatise, *On Original Sin*, laid the groundwork for later Reformed treatises (see *Saint Augustin's Anti-Pelagian Works*, translated by Peter Holmes and Robert Wallis and revised by Benjamin B. Warfield, *Nicene and Post-Nicene Fathers*, edited by Philip Schaff [Grand Rapids: Eerdmans, 1991], First Series, Volume 5, pp. 237-257).

Jonathan Edwards, *Original Sin*, Volume 3 of *The Works of Jonathan Edwards*, edited by Clyde A. Holbrook (1758; New Haven: Yale, 1970), is *the* Calvinistic classic on the subject. Pastors need to familiarize themselves with this treatment if they are to preach effectively against the moral and theological drift of today. The best secondary source on the Edwardsean view is C. Samuel Storms, *Tragedy in Eden: Original Sin in the Theology of Jonathan Edwards* (Lanham, MD: University Press of America, 1985). Storms concludes that there are weaknesses in Edwards's argument that move toward a "system of constitutional depravity and strict volitional determinism [that] inevitably makes God the author of sin."

For an able nineteenth-century work, see Henry Augustus Boardman's *A Treatise on the Scripture Doctrine of Original Sin* (Philadelphia: Presbyterian Board of Publication, 1839). Boardman was the renowned minister of Philadelphia's Tenth Presbyterian Church. This work established his reputation as an upholder and defender of Old School Presbyterian theology.

For a thorough twentieth-century Reformed treatment of Romans 5:12-19, read John Murray, *The Imputation of Adam's Sin* (Grand Rapids: Eerdmans, 1959). Murray, who prefers the term *imputed sin* rather than *original sin,* definitively refutes Pelagian and Roman Catholic views of original sin. He clarifies the *realistic* approach to original sin as advocated by William Shedd and Augustus

Strong, but pleads for the *representative* or *federalist* view. The best, brief article on the imputation of sin is Benjamin B. Warfield, "Imputation," in *Biblical and Theological Studies*, edited by Samuel Craig (Philadelphia: Presbyterian and Reformed, 1968), pp. 262-269.

American theologians have done much of the important theological debate on the doctrine of original sin. For the tensions in American theology on this critical, yet often neglected doctrine, see H. Shelton Smith, *Changing Conceptions of Original Sin: A Study in American Theology Since 1750* (New York: Scribners, 1955); Gary D. Long, "The Doctrine of Original Sin in New England Theology from Jonathan Edwards to Edwards Amasa Park" (Th.D. dissertation, Dallas Theological Seminary, 1972); George P. Hutchinson, *The Problem of Original Sin in American Presbyterian Theology* (Philadelphia: Presbyterian and Reformed, 1972). Hutchinson is the most helpful. His short, lucid work on original sin is written from a historical and theological perspective, and covers American theologians from Jonathan Edwards through John Murray. This is the best introduction to the issues at stake in the doctrine of original sin.

Other historical studies on original sin worthy of being mentioned (though not written from a Reformed perspective) include Henri Rondet, *Original Sin: The Patristic and Theological Background*, translated by Cajetan Finegan (Staten Island: Alba House, 1972), and G. Vandervelde, *Original Sin: Two Major Trends in Contemporary Roman Catholic Interpretation* (Amsterdam: Rodopi, 1975).

For the dread consequences of original sin, no work is more powerful than Thomas Goodwin, *An Unregenerate Man's Guiltiness Before God in Respect of Sin and Punishment*, Volume 10 of *The Works of Thomas Goodwin* (Edinburgh: James Nichol, 1865; reprint Eureka, CA: Tanski, 1996). See also Gerrit C. Berkouwer's probing 600-page work, *Sin*, translated by Phillip C. Holtrop (Grand Rapids: Eerdmans, 1971). Berkouwer is particularly helpful on the relationship of sin to the law (Chapter 6) and to the gospel (Chapter 7). Also helpful on most issues is Bernard L. Ramm, *Offense to Reason: A Theology of Sin* (New York: Harper & Row, 1985).

For additional books on mankind's fall in Paradise, see notes on Article 14.

ARTICLE 16

Predestination: Election and Reprobation

The best pre-Reformation writing on predestination is Augustine's "On the Predestination of the Saints," in *Nicene and Post-Nicene Fathers of the Christian Church,* First Series, Volume 5, edited by Philip Schaff (reprint Grand Rapids: Eerdmans, 1975), pp. 493-520. For a secondary source on Augustine, consult J. B. Mozley, *A Treatise on the Augustinian Doctrine of Predestination* (New York: E.P. Dutton, 1878). For a secondary source on the views of several of the major theologians of the ancient church (including Augustine, Chapter 7), see George Stanley Faber, *The Primitive Doctrine of Election* (New York: Charles Henley, 1840). Faber also covers the Reformation period on predestination.

The great Reformation theologian on predestination was, of course, John Calvin. For a concise treatment of his views, read *Institutes of the Christian Religion,* edited by John T. McNeill, translated by Ford Lewis Battles (Philadelphia: Westminster Press, 1960), Book 3, Chapters 21-24. For Calvin's most polemical, extended treatment of predestination, see *Concerning the Eternal Predestination of God,* translated by J.K.S. Reid (London: James Clarke, 1961; a lesser translation of this work is also taken up in *Calvin's Calvinism,* translated by Henry Cole [1856; reprint Grand Rapids: Reformed Free, 1991]). Also see *Thirteene Sermons of Maister Iohn Calvine, Entreating of the Free Election of God in Jacob and of Reprobation in Esau* (London, 1579; reprinted as *Sermons on Election and Reprobation* [Audubon, NJ: Old Paths, 1996]). Though predestination is not a dominant theme in Calvin, valuable material on the doctrine can be found in many of his commentaries, sermons, treatises, and letters.

Secondary sources on Calvin's doctrine of predestination are numerous. For a succinct, able treatment, see *Collected Writings of John Murray* (Edinburgh: Banner of Truth Trust, 1982), 4:191-204. The best, most balanced work on Calvinian predestination, however, is Fred H. Klooster, *Calvin's Doctrine of Predestination* (Grand Rapids: Baker, 1977). Klooster successfully argues that for Calvin election is always sovereign and gracious; reprobation, always sovereign and just. Two older, important articles are Theodore F. Herman, "Calvin's Doctrine of Predestination," *Reformed Church Review* 13 (1909):183-208; S. Leigh Hunt, "Predestination in the Institutes of John Calvin," *Evangelical Quarterly* 9 (1937):38-45. Significant, unpublished dissertations include Mcknight Crawford Cowper, "Calvin's Doctrine of Predestination and its Ethical Consequences" (Ph.D., Union Theological Seminary, 1942); George Hupp DeHority, "Calvin's Doctrine of Predestination: Criticisms and Reinterpretations" (Ph.D., Union Theological Seminary, 1948); John Weeks, "A Comparison of Calvin and Edwards on the Doctrine of Election" (Ph.D., University of Chicago, 1963); David F. Wells, "*Decretum dei speciale*: An Analysis of the Content and Significance of Calvin's Doctrine of Soteriological Predestination" (Th.M., Trinity Evangelical Divinity, 1967); David N. Wiley, "Calvin's Doctrine of Predestination: His Principal Soteriological and Polemical Doctrine" (Ph.D., Duke University, 1971). Of these dissertations, Wiley's and Wells's are the most helpful.

Other Reformers also wrote classics on predestination. The most famous work is Hieronymous Zanchius, *Absolute Predestination* (reprint Grand Rapids: Sovereign Grace, 1971). Unfortunately, contemporary reprints use the edition produced by Augustus Toplady, who liberally sprinkled comments throughout the volume without proper footnotes.

The best secondary source defending the position that the Reformers were united on the doctrine of predestination (despite the differences of some from Calvin in methodology) is Richard Muller, *Christ and the Decree: Christology and Predestination in Reformed Theology from Calvin to Perkins* (Grand Rapids: Baker, 1988). This volume is a substantial revision of an excellent dissertation, "Predestination and Christology in Sixteenth Century Reformed Theology" (Ph.D., Duke University, 1976). Other helpful writings on the predestinarian views of Calvin's successor, Theodore Beza, and other Calvinists include Benjamin B. Warfield, "Predestination in the Reformed Confessions," *The Presbyterian and Reformed Review* 12 (1901):49-128 (reprinted in *Studies in Theology*); Harry Buis, *Historic Protestantism and Predestination* (Philadelphia: Presbyterian and Reformed, 1958); John Murray, "Calvin, Dort, and Westminster on Predestination: A Comparative Study," in *Crisis in the Reformed Churches: Essays in Commemoration of the Great Synod of Dort, 1618-1619,* edited by Peter Y. DeJong (Grand Rapids: Reformed Fellowship, 1968; reprinted in *Collected Writings*, 4:205-215); John S. Bray, *Theodore Beza's Doctrine of Predestination* (Nieuwkoop: B. DeGraaf, 1975); Herman Hanko, "Predestination in Calvin, Beza, and Later Reformed Theology," *Protestant Reformed Theological Journal* X, 2 (1977): 1-24; Paul Helm, *Calvin and the Calvinists* (Edinburgh: Banner of Truth, 1982); Donald W. Sinnema, "The Issue of Reprobation at the Synod of Dort (1618-19) in Light of the History of This Doctrine" (Ph.D. dissertation, University of St. Michael's College, 1985).

For the views of the English Reformers, see O. T. Hargrave, "The Doctrine of Predestination in the English Reformation" (Ph.D. dissertation, Vanderbilt University, 1966).

For the English Puritans, see "A Christian and Plain Treatise on the Manner and Order of Predestination, and of the Largeness of God's Grace," in *The Works of William Perkins* (London: John Legate, 1609), 2:687-730; "Reprobation Asserted," in *The Works of John Bunyan*, edited by George Offor (1859; reprint Edinburgh: Banner of Truth Trust, 1994), 2:335-58; Anthony Burgess, *Spiritual Refining* (1652; reprint Ames, IA: International Outreach, 1990), pp. 643-74. For secondary sources, consult Dewey D. Wallace, Jr., *Puritans and Predestination: Grace in English Protestant Theology, 1525-1695* (Chapel Hill, NC: University of North Carolina, 1982); Iain Murray, "The Puritans and the Doctrine of Election," in *The Wisdom of our Fathers* (Puritan Conference, 1956), pp. 1-13.

For a reliable eighteenth-century book on predestination, see William Cooper, *The Doctrine of Predestination unto Life Explained and Vindicated* (London: Dilly, 1765). One of the best nineteenth-century works is James H. Thornwell, *Election and Reprobation* (1871; reprinted in *The Collected Writings* [Edinburgh: Banner of

Truth Trust, 1974], 2:105-203). See also Charles Hodge, *Systematic Theology* (New York: Scribner, Armstrong, & Co., 1877), 2:313-353.

The most basic, reliable, and readable twentieth-century works on predestination are Loraine Boettner, *The Reformed Doctrine of Predestination* (1932; reprinted Philadelphia: Presbyterian and Reformed, 1968); Gordon H. Clark, *Biblical Predestination* (Nutley, NJ: Presbyterian and Reformed, 1969); Arthur W. Pink, *The Doctrines of Election and Justification* (Grand Rapids: Baker, 1974); John H. Gerstner, *A Predestination Primer* (Winona Lake, IN: Alpha, 1979); C. Samuel Storms, *Chosen for Life: An Introductory Guide to the Doctrine of Election* (Grand Rapids: Baker, 1987). Gerrit C. Berkouwer, *Divine Election*, translated by Hugo Bekker (Grand Rapids: Eerdmans, 1960), is imbalanced on election and weak on reprobation, as has been pointed out in Alvin L. Baker, *Berkouwer's Doctrine of Election: Balance or Imbalance?* (Phillipsburg, NJ: Presbyterian and Reformed, 1981). Although unreliable in many of his other writings, Paul K. Jewett is at his best in *Election and Predestination* (Grand Rapids: Eerdmans, 1985). He firmly rejects Karl Barth's interpretation, and sees the appropriate response to the awesomeness of divine sovereignty as worship.

Where should you begin? Read and study John 6:37-44, Romans 9-11, Ephesians 1, and all the texts listed in *Nave's Topical Bible* that affirm predestination. Then read Calvin's *Institutes*, 3.21-24, Chapter 3 of the Westminster Confession of Faith, the first head of the Canons of Dort, and finally, Boettner or Storms.

ARTICLE 17

God Promises Salvation in Christ to Fallen Man

The Promises of God in General

Having already noted sources on the fall and misery of man (see Articles 14 and 15), only works related to the promises of God in Christ Jesus need to be noted here. Concerning the personal application of the promises of God, the most helpful book is by William Spurstowe, *The Wells of Salvation Opened: or A Treatise discovering the nature, preciousness, and usefullness, of the Gospel Promises, and Rules for the Right Application of them* (London: T. R. & E. M. for Ralph Smith, 1655). Unfortunately, this work has not been reprinted since 1821. Its biblical, doctrinal, experiential, and practical substance and balance are consistent with the best of the Puritan tradition. Two additional, valuable writings on receiving the promises of God are Andrew Gray, "Great and Precious Promises," in *The Works of the Reverend and Pious Andrew Gray* (1839; reprint Morgan, PA: Soli Deo Gloria, 1992), pp. 115-168; and Robert Brown, "The Application of the Holy Scriptures," in *Doctrinal and Experimental Theology* (London: William Wileman, 1899), pp. 113-153. Herbert W. Lockyer, *All the Promises of the Bible* (Grand Rapids: Zondervan, 1962) is too brief and simplistic to be of much help, but it could be used for devotional reading.

Messianic Promises in Particular

The best Puritan work in this field is Thomas Taylor, *Christ Revealed: or The Old Testament Explained; A Treatise of the Types and Shadowes of our Savior* (London: M. F. for R. Dawlman and L. Fawne, 1635; reprint Delmar, NY: Scholars' Facsimiles & Reprints, 1979).

Several good, late-nineteenth-century works focus on the messianic promises of the Old Testament. Ernst W. Hengstenberg,

Christology of the Old Testament and a Commentary on the Messianic Predictions, 4 volumes (1872-1878; reprint Grand Rapids: Kregel, 1956) is a valuable study of Old Testament promises, types, and prophecies of Christ. Also helpful are Alfred Edersheim, *Prophecy and History in Relation to the Messiah* (New York: Randolph, 1885); Caspar Von Orelli, *The Old Testament Prophecy of the Consummation of God's Kingdom* (Edinburgh: T. & T. Clark, 1889); David Baron, *Rays of Messiah's Glory: Christ in the Old Testament* (1895; reprint Winona Lake, IN: Alpha, 1979). Two virtually unobtainable works were reprinted in one volume in 1983 as *The Messianic Prophecies* by Klock & Klock (of Minneapolis): Franz Delitzch, *The Messianic Prophecies in Historical Succession* (Edinburgh: T. & T. Clark, 1891) offers a series of famous lectures designed to reawaken interest in some long-neglected Old Testament passages; Paton J. Gloag, *Messianic Prophecies* (Edinburgh: T. & T. Clark, 1879) offers a series of Baird lectures delivered at the University of Glasgow.

The most exhaustive twentieth-century work is Gerard Van Groningen, *Messianic Revelation in the Old Testament* (Grand Rapids: Baker, 1990), which traces in more than a thousand pages the messianic expectation progressively revealed in the Hebrew Scriptures. Van Groningen has included an extensive bibliography of books and articles for additional study. Herbert W. Lockyer, *All the Messianic Prophecies of the Bible* (Grand Rapids: Zondervan, 1962) is devotional in nature and covers even more prophecies than Van Groningen. But it lacks careful exegesis and depth.

Recent studies that view the entire Old Testament from the perspective of God's covenantal promises in Christ include Walter C. Kaiser, Jr., *Toward an Old Testament Theology* (Grand Rapids: Zondervan, 1978); O. Palmer Robertson, *The Christ of the Covenants* (Nutley, NJ: Presbyterian and Reformed, 1980); Thomas E. McComiskey, *The Covenants of Promise: A Theology of the Old Testament Covenants* (Grand Rapids: Baker, 1985).

For an easy, edifying read, try Edmund P. Clowney, *The Unfolding Mystery: Discovering Christ in the Old Testament* (Colorado Springs: NavPress, 1988).

The Recovery of Fallen Man

Concerning the overall theme of the recovery of fallen man through the Mediator, no work surpasses that of Thomas Goodwin, *Christ our Mediator* (reprint Grand Rapids: Sovereign Grace, 1971;

reprinted as Volume 5 in *The Works of Thomas Goodwin* [Eureka, CA: Tanski, 1996]). It ably expounds primary New Testament texts on the mediatorship of Christ. Goodwin is particularly enlightening on his exposition of several key passages from Hebrews (2:14-17; 4:14-16; 10:3-10, 19-22; 13:20-21). His intelligent piety and experimental depth promotes clarity of thought and warmth of soul.

ARTICLE 18
The Incarnation

The oldest classic on the incarnation is Athanasius, *The Incarnation of the Word of God* (London: A.R. Mowbray and Co., 1963), in which the author, unquestionably the best theologian of his day, uses arguments based on the incarnation to refute Arianism. For representative patristic texts that treat the doctrine of incarnation, see E. R. Hardy, *Christology of the Later Fathers*, Volume 3 (Philadelphia: Westminster, 1954), and R. A. Norris, *The Christological Controversy* (Philadelphia: Fortress, 1980).

For a Reformed treatment, consult Calvin's *Institutes*, Book 2, Chapters 12-14, and Christological writings by Reformed theologians such as Charles Hodge, B. B. Warfield, Louis Berkhof, and John Murray.

Two nineteenth-century works by Edwin H. Gifford and Samuel J. Andrews were reprinted in one volume as *The Incarnation of Christ* (Minneapolis: Klock & Klock, 1981). Gifford discusses Philippians 2:5-11 with theological acumen and Andrews ably discourses on the necessity of Christ's humanity. M. F. Sadler, *Emmanuel, Or, The Incarnation of the Son of God the Foundation of Immutable Truth* (New York: Scribner, Welford, & Co., 1866) shows how the doctrine of incarnation impinges on the whole of Christology. William M. Ramsay, *Was Christ Born at Bethlehem?* (London: Hodder and Stoughton, 1898) concentrates on the enrollment of Quirinius and, in the process, provides a rather formal and dry defense of the accuracy of Luke's gospel on the birth of Jesus. J. J. Van Oosterzee, *The Person and Work of the Redeemer*, translated by Maurice J. Evans (London: Hodder and Stoughton, 1886) contains a helpful chapter on the voluntary character of Christ's incarnation.

For a scholarly defense of the supernatural conception of

Christ, see J. Gresham Machen's timely treatment, *The Virgin Birth of Christ* (1930; reprint Grand Rapids: Baker, 1967). Also, consult Howard A. Hanke, *The Validity of the Virgin Birth* (Grand Rapids: Zondervan, 1963) and C. F. D. Moule, *The Origin of Christology* (Cambridge: Cambridge University Press, 1977), both of which complement Machen's work. Leon Morris, *The Story of the Christ Child* (Grand Rapids: Eerdmans, 1960) combines scholarship and devotion in expounding the nativity stories in Matthew and Luke. Charles Lee Feinberg, *Is the Virgin Birth in the Old Testament?* (Whittier, CA: Emeth, 1967) includes helpful studies on Genesis 3:14-15, Isaiah 7:14, and Jeremiah 31:22. Robert G. Gromacki, *The Virgin Birth* (Nashville: Nelson, 1974) dispels popular misinterpretations of Christ's conception and birth.

The best recent books on Christ incarnate are David F. Wells, *The Person of Christ: A Biblical and Historical Analysis of the Incarnation* (1984; reprint Alliance, OH: Bible Scholar Books, 1992), and Millard J. Erickson, *The Word Became Flesh: A Contemporary Incarnational Christology* (Grand Rapids: Baker, 1991). Wells's book is neatly divided into three sections: biblical foundations, historical development, and modern interpretation. Justice is done to each section. Of Erickson's work, J. I. Packer says, "Erickson shows convincingly that an incarnational Christology of classic Chalcedonian type remains possible and natural today, and fits the biblical data better than any other."

Where should you begin? Read Machen.

ARTICLE 19
Christ's Two Natures in One Person

Read the Chalcedonian Creed, which provided the entire Christian church with a standard of Christological orthodoxy in declaring that Christ's two natures exist "without confusion, without change, without division, without separation" (see *The Seven Ecumenical Councils*, edited by Henry R. Percival, in *Nicene and Post-Nicene Fathers*, edited by Philip Schaff and Henry Wace, 2nd series [1899; reprint Grand Rapids: Eerdmans, 1991], Vol. 14, pp. 243-296; also, R. V. Sellers, *The Council of Chalcedon: A Historical and Doctrinal Survey* [London: SPCK, 1953], and A. Grillmeier, *Christ in Christian Tradition* [Atlanta: John Knox, 1975], pp. 520-557). Read, too, the Chalcedonian-based Athanasian Creed, Articles 29-43.

The best seventeenth-century work on Christ's two natures in one person is John Owen, *A Declaration of the Glorious Mystery of the Person of Christ* (1679), reprinted in Volume 1 of the Goold edition of Owen's *Works* (London: Banner of Truth Trust, 1965).

A. B. Bruce, *The Humiliation of Christ* (1876; reprint New York: George H. Doran, 1898) is a widely used study of Christ's state of humiliation based on Philippians 2:5-8 and other passages. Also helpful is Bruce's historical survey of the interpretation of this doctrine from the Council of Chalcedon to Schleiermacher.

For standard evangelical works on the basic issues involved in the doctrine of Christ's two natures in one person, see Nathan E. Wood, *The Person and Work of Jesus Christ* (Philadelphia: American Baptist Publication Society, 1908); Hugh Ross Mackintosh, *The Doctrine of the Person of Christ* (Edinburgh: T. and T. Clark, 1914); Loraine Boettner, *The Person of Christ* (Grand Rapids: Eerdmans, 1943); Leon Morris, *The Lord from Heaven* (London: InterVarsity

Press, 1958). Of those treatments, Boettner's is the simplest and most Reformed guide.

For a deeper discussion, read Benjamin B. Warfield, *The Person and Work of Christ*, edited by Samuel G. Craig (Philadelphia: Presbyterian and Reformed, 1950) and the companion volumes by Gerrit C. Berkouwer, *The Person of Christ* and *The Work of Christ* (Grand Rapids: Eerdmans, 1954, 1965). Warfield's massive volume, second only to Owen's, sets forth the doctrine of Christ exegetically and polemically. Composed in the context of the so-called "quest for the historical Jesus," Warfield stresses that the only Jesus discoverable in the New Testament is a supernatural person. He maintains that it is "the desupernaturalized Jesus which is the mythical Jesus, who never had any existence, the postulation of whose existence explains nothing and leaves the whole historical development hanging in the air."

Berkouwer's volumes discuss the historical pronouncements of the ecumenical councils and the Reformed confessions as well as the nature, unity, and sinlessness of Christ. They provide an in-depth discussion of Christ's work in the states of humiliation and exaltation. While Berkouwer is fully abreast of current theological literature, he is too often influenced by it, and takes a position too moderate or vague on many issues. The value of Berkouwer lies in his grasp of Reformed thinkers and presentation of issues in theology. He asks and begins to answer some of the most difficult questions.

For books that focus on the divinity of Jesus, see Article 10.

ARTICLE 20
Justice and Mercy in Christ

No Reformed confessional statement deals with the justice and mercy of God in Christ unto salvation more biblically, poignantly, and experientially than the Heidelberg Catechism in Questions 9-18. Begin here, then read sermons, commentaries, and works on the Heidelberg Catechism. Though sources for the Heidelberg Catechism are most common in Dutch, adequate works are available in English. Consult the following chronological list:

Olevian, Caspar. *An Exposition of the Symbol of the Apostles, or rather of the articles of faith. In which the chiefe points of the everlasting and free covenant between God and the faithful are briefly and plainly handled. Gathered out of the catechizing sermons of Caspar Olevian.* Translated by Iohn Fielde. London: H. Middleton, 1581.

Bastingius, Jeremias. *An Exposition or Commentarie upon the Catechisme of Christian Religion which is taught in the Schooles and churches both of the Lowe Countryes and of the dominions of the Countie Palatine.* Cambridge: John Legatt, 1589.

Ames, William. *The Substance of Christian Religion; Or a plain and easie Draught of the Christian Catechisme in LII Lectures.* London: T. Mabb for T. Davies, 1659.

Witte, Petrus de. *Catechizing upon the Heidelbergh Catechisme of the Reformed Christian Religion.* Translated for the English Reformed Congregation in Amsterdam. Amsterdam: Gillis Joosten Saeghman, 1662.

Ronde, Lambertus de. *A System Containing the Principles of the Christian Religion, Suitable to the Heidelberg Catechism.* New York, 1763.

Vander Kemp, John. *The Christian Entirely the Property of Christ, in Life and Death. Fifty-three sermons on the Heidelberg Catechism wherein the doctrine of faith, received in the Reformed Church, is defended against the principal opponents, and the practical improvement and direction of it to evangelical piety, enforced.* 2 vols. Translated by John M. Van Harlingen. New Brunswick, NJ: Abraham Blauvelt, 1810.

Fisher, Samuel Reed. *Exercises on the Heidelberg Catechism adapted to the use of Sabbath Schools and Catechetical Classes.* Chambersburg, PA: Publication office of the German Reformed Church, 1844.

Ursinus, Zacharias. *The Commentary of Dr. Zacharias Ursinus on the Heidelberg Catechism.* Translated by George W. Williard. Columbus: Scott & Bascom, 1852.

Bethune, George Washington. *Expository Lectures on the Heidelberg Catechism.* 2 vols. New York: Sheldon & Co., 1864.

Whitmer, Adam Carl. *Notes on the Heidelberg Catechism: for Parents, Teachers and Catechumens.* Philadelphia: Grant, Faires & Rodgers, 1878.

Thelemann, Otto. *An Aid to the Heidelberg Catechism.* Translated by Rev. M. Peters. Reading, PA: James I. Good, 1896.

Richards, George. *Studies on the Heidelberg Catechism.* Philadelphia: Publication and Sunday School Board of the Reformed Church in the United States, 1913.

Kuiper, Henry J., ed. *Sermons on the Heidelberg Catechism.* 5 vols. Grand Rapids: Zondervan, 1936-1956.

Van Baalen, Jan Karel. *The Heritage of the Fathers, A Commentary on the Heidelberg Catechism.* Grand Rapids: Eerdmans, 1948.

Van Reenen, G. *The Heidelberg Catechism: Explained for the Humble and Sincere in Fifty-two Sermons.* Paterson, NJ: Lont & Overkamp, 1955.

Vis, Jean. *We Are the Lord's.* Grand Rapids: Society for Reformed Publications, 1955.

Bruggink, Donald J., ed. *Guilt, Grace and Gratitude: A Commentary on the Heidelberg Catechism commemorating its 400th Anniversary.* New York: Half Moon Press, 1963.

Kersten, Gerrit Hendrik. *The Heidelberg Catechism in 52 Sermons.* 2 vols. Translated by Gertrude DeBruyn and Cornelius Quist. Grand Rapids: Netherlands Reformed Congregations, 1968.

Josse, James, ed. *Sermons on the Heidelberg Catechism.* Grand Rapids: Board of Publication of the Christian Reformed Church, 1970.

Hoeksema, Herman. *The Triple Knowledge, An Exposition of the Heidelberg Catechism.* 3 vols. Grand Rapids: Reformed Free Publishing Association, 1970-1972.

Jones, Norman L. *Study Helps on the Heidelberg Catechism.* Eureka, SD: Publication Committee of the Eureka Classis, Reformed Church in the United States, 1981.

Praamsma, Louis. *Before the Face of God: A Study of the Heidelberg Catechism.* 2 vols. Jordan Station, Ontario: Paideia Press, 1987.

DeJong, Peter Y., and Kloosterman, Nelson D., eds. *That Christ May Dwell in Your Hearts. Sermons on the Heidelberg Catechism, Lord's Days 1-20.* Orange City, IA: Mid-American Reformed Seminary, 1988.

Klooster, Fred H. *A Mighty Comfort: The Christian Faith According to the Heidelberg Catechism.* Grand Rapids: CRC Publications, 1990.

Stam, Clarence. *Living in the Joy of Faith: The Christian Faith as outlined in the Heidelberg Catechism.* Neerlandia, Alberta: Inheritance, 1991.

Heerschap, M. *Zion's Comfort in Life and Death: Fifty-two Sermons on the Heidelberg Catechism.* 2 vols. Lethbridge, Alberta: Netherlands Reformed Congregation, 1992-94.

Olevianus, Caspar. *A Firm Foundation: An Aid to Interpreting the Heidelberg Catechism.* Translated by Lyle D. Bierma. Grand Rapids: Baker, 1995.

Beeke, Joel R. "Heidelberg Catechism Sermons." 5 vols. Jordan, Ontario: Heritage Reformed Church, 1998.

Of those authors, most helpful on the relationship of justice and mercy are Ursinus, Olevianus, Thelemann, Kersten, and Hoeksema.

ARTICLE 21

Salvation in Christ as High Priest

Article 21 of the Belgic Confession merges three Christological themes: the suffering Christ, the priestly Christ, the atoning Christ.

Christ in His Sufferings
   No work on Christ's suffering begs reprinting more than that of James Durham, *Christ Crucified; or, The Marrow of the Gospel in 72 Sermons on Isaiah 53,* 2 vols. (1683; reprint Glasgow: Alex Adam, 1792). Of these sermons, Spurgeon rightly notes: "This is marrow indeed. We need say no more; Durham is a prince among spiritual expositors." John Brown, *The Sufferings and Glories of the Messiah* (New York: Robert Carter, 1853) also offers a solid, exegetical, and practical exposition of Psalm 18 and Isaiah 52:13 through 53:12.
   No volume on Christ's sufferings, however, surpasses that of the great German Reformed writer, Friedrich W. Krummacher. *The Suffering Saviour* (1856; reprint Chicago: Moody Press, 1966), which is warmly personal, instructive, and experiential, is worthy of multiple readings. At times Krummacher's exegesis is faulty and his imagination too picturesque, but those weaknesses scarcely tarnish this unparalleled treatise.
   The greatest twentieth-century work on Christ's sufferings is the *magnum opus* of Klaas Schilder, *Christ in His Suffering; Christ on Trial; Christ Crucified*, translated by Henry Zylstra, 3 vols. (1938-40; reprint Minneapolis: Klock and Klock, 1978). Schilder's "Lenten trilogy" is often profound and contains much food for meditation. Unfortunately, however, these volumes are marred by speculation and philosophical tendencies not based on exegetical evidence. The best one-volume twentieth-century work is Herman Hoeksema, *When I Survey...: A Lenten Anthology* (Grand Rapids: Reformed Free, 1977). A single, basic theme underlies each of six sections that were

originally published as books of radio messages (1943-56) titled *The Amazing Cross, The Royal Sufferer, The Power of the Cross, Rejected of Men, Jesus in the Midst,* and *Man of Sorrows.* Erich H. Kiehl, *The Passion of Our Lord* (Grand Rapids: Baker, 1990) focuses on the last week of Christ's sufferings. It offers copious insights from historical and archaeological sources.

Christ as High Priest

There are not many good, Reformed books on Christ as High Priest. The best is H. H. Meeter, *The Heavenly High Priesthood of Christ: An Exegetico-Dogmatic Study* (Grand Rapids: Eerdmans-Sevensma, 1916). Note especially Chapters 4-5 on Christ as a priest after the order of Melchizedek. George Stevenson, *Treatise on the Offices of Christ* (Edinburgh: W. P. Kennedy, 1845), a noteworthy Anglican work on the offices of Christ, includes a helpful section on Christ's priestly work. J. C. Philpot is at his best in *Meditations on the Sacred Humanity of the Blessed Redeemer* (1859-60; reprint Harpenden, Herts: O. G. Pearce, 1975), which includes three experimental chapters on Christ as the "great High Priest." The most recent, soundly Reformed work that covers Christ's threefold office with a particular focus on his atoning priestly work is Robert Letham, *The Work of Christ* (Downers Grove, IL: InterVarsity Press, 1993). Letham is particularly helpful in discussing the viewpoints of significant Christian thinkers, from the church fathers to contemporary theologians.

Christ's Atonement

The best and most prolific Reformed treatments on the atonement of Christ were produced in the last half of the nineteenth century. They include Charles Hodge, *The Orthodox Doctrine Regarding the Extent of the Atonement Vindicated* (Edinburgh, 1846); Francis Turretin, *The Atonement of Christ,* translated by James R. Willson (1859; reprint Grand Rapids: Baker, 1978); Robert Smith Candlish, *The Atonement: Its Reality, Completeness, and Extent* (London: T. Nelson, 1861); Archibald Alexander Hodge, *The Atonement* (1867; reprint Grand Rapids: Baker, 1975); George Smeaton, *The Doctrine of the Atonement as Taught by Jesus Christ Himself* (1868; reprint Edinburgh: Banner of Truth, 1992); George Smeaton, *The Doctrine of the Atonement as Taught by the Apostles* (1870; reprint Edinburgh: Banner of Truth, 1992); Thomas Jackson Crawford, *The Doctrine of*

Holy Scripture Respecting the Atonement (1871; reprint Grand Rapids: Baker, 1954); Hugh Martin, *The Atonement* (1882; reprint Edinburgh: John Knox Press, 1976); Robert L. Dabney, *Christ Our Penal Substitute* (1898; reprint Harrisonburg, VA: Sprinkle, 1985).

For good, basic, twentieth-century treatments of the atonement from a Reformed perspective, read Louis Berkhof, *Vicarious Atonement Through Christ* (Grand Rapids: Eerdmans, 1936) and Rienk B. Kuiper, *For Whom Did Christ Die?* (1959; reprint Grand Rapids: Baker, 1982). Berkhof and Kuiper offer the best introduction to the doctrine of the atonement.

For historical studies on the atonement, see William Cunningham, *Historical Theology* (1862; reprint London: Banner of Truth, 1960), Vol. 2, pp. 237-370; G. C. Foley, *Anselm's Theory of the Atonement* (London, 1909); H. Rashdall, *The Idea of Atonement in Christian Theology* (London: Macmillan, 1919); Dorus Paul Rudisill, *The Doctrine of the Atonement in Jonathan Edwards and His Successors* (New York: Poseidon, 1971).

For additional material on the above doctrines, consult traditional, Reformed systematic theologies and the bibliographical notes in articles 10, 18, and 19. For an edifying work that summarizes the Christological doctrines covered in Article 21, see Philip Henry, *Christ All in All, or What Christ is Made to Believers* (reprint Swengel, PA: Reiner, 1970). In the three centuries since this book was published by the father of the well-known commentator, Matthew Henry, its forty-one chapters (which expound Colossians 3:11) have lost none of their power to move the heart and motivate the mind.

ARTICLE 22

Salvation by Faith in Christ Alone

To understand the ancient church's teaching on salvation by faith, see Clement of Alexandria, *Miscellanies* (2.1-6, 11-12; 5.1); Ambrose, *On the Faith*; Augustine, *On the Value of Believing* and *On Faith in Things Not Seen*. For a secondary source, consult H. A. Wolfson, *Philosophy of the Church Fathers* (Cambridge: Harvard, 1956), pp. 102-140.

For Reformation writers, consult *Luther's Works*, edited by J. Pelikan, et al., 55 vols. (St. Louis: Concordia, Vols. 1-30; Philadelphia: Fortress Press, Vols. 31-55, 1955-79), and Calvin's *Institutes of the Christian Religion* (Philadelphia: Westminster Press, 1960), Book 3, Chapters 2-3. Norman Shepherd provides a succinct summary of one Reformer's view in "Zanchius on Saving Faith," *Westminster Theological Journal* 36 (1973):31-47.

The Puritans excelled in writing on the doctrine of saving faith in Christ from a scriptural and experiential perspective. Significant titles in print or fairly accessible include Jonathan Edwards, "Justification by Faith Alone," in *Works of Jonathan Edwards*, ed. Edward Hickman, Vol. 1, pp. 620-654 (1834; reprint Edinburgh: Banner of Truth Trust, 1974); Thomas Goodwin, "The Object and Acts of Justifying Faith," in *The Works of Thomas Goodwin, D.D.*, ed. John Miller, Vol. 8 (1865; reprint Edinburgh: Banner of Truth Trust, 1988); Andrew Gray, *The Mystery of Faith Opened Up: Or, some Sermons Concerning Faith* (Edinburgh: Andrew Anderson, 1697 [reprinted in *The Works of the Reverend and Pious Andrew Gray* (1813; Ligonier, PA: Soli Deo Gloria, 1992)]; John Owen, "The Doctrine of Justification by Faith" (1677), in *The Works of John Owen*, ed. William H. Goold, Vol. 5, pp. 1-400 (1851; reprint Edinburgh: Banner of Truth Trust,

1976); John Preston, *The Breast-Plate of Faith and Love*, 5th ed. (1632; reprint Edinburgh: Banner of Truth Trust, 1979); Robert Traill, "A Vindication of the Protestant Doctrine Concerning Justification," in *The Works of the late Reverend Robert Traill*, Vol. 1, pp. 252-96 (1810; reprint Edinburgh: Banner of Truth Trust, 1975).

Listed chronologically, scarce Puritan works on faith include Thomas Wilson, *A Dialogve About Ivstification by Faith* (London: W. Hall for N. Butter, 1610); Miles Mosse, *Ivstifying and Saving Faith Distingvished from the faith of the Deuils* (Cambridge: Cantrell Legse, 1614); John Rogers, *The Doctrine of Faith: wherein are particularly handled twelve Principall Points, which explaine the Nature and Vse of it* (London: for N. Newbery and H. Overton, 1629); Ezekiel Culverwell, *A Treatise of Faith: Wherein is Declared How a Man May Live by Faith, and Find Relief in all His Necessities* (London: I. D. for Hen: Overton, 1633); John Downame, *A Treatise of the True Nature and Definition of Justifying Faith* (Oxford: I. Lichfield for E. Forrest, 1635); John Cotton, *The Way of Faith* (1643; reprint New York: AMS Press, 1983); Samuel Rutherford, *The Trial and Triumph of Faith* (1645; reprint Edinburgh: William Collins, 1845); Matthew Lawrence, *The Use and Practice of Faith: or, Faiths Vniversal Vsefulness, and Quickning Influence into every Kinde and Degree of the Christian Life* (London: A. Maxey for Willian, 1657); Robert Dixon, *The Doctrine of Faith, Justification, and Assurance* (London: William Godbid, 1668); Edward Polhill, *Precious Faith* (London: Thomas Cockerill, 1675); Thomas Cole, *A Discourse of Regeneration, Faith, and Repentance* (London: for Thomas Cockerill, 1689).

The best eighteenth-century works on faith are James Fraser, *A Treatise concerning Justifying and Saving Faith* (Edinburgh: John Mosman and Company, 1722), and the well-known classic by William Romaine, *The Life, Walk and Triumph of Faith* (1765; reprint London: James Clarke, 1970), which stresses the need to trust the divinity of Christ and to walk by faith in subjection to the Word of God.

For historical-theological, twentieth-century studies on faith, see Geoffrey F. Nuttall, *The Holy Spirit in Puritan Faith and Experience* (1946; reprint Chicago: University of Chicago Press, 1992); David Broughton Knox, *The Doctrine of Faith in the Reign of Henry VIII* (London: James Clarke, 1961); Robert Letham, "Saving Faith and Assurance in Reformed Theology: Zwingli to the Synod of Dort," 2 vols. (Ph.D. dissertation, University of Aberdeen, 1979); Victor A.

Shepherd, *The Nature and Function of Faith in the Theology of John Calvin* (Macon, GA: Mercer University Press, 1983); Joel R. Beeke, *Assurance of Faith: Calvin, English Puritanism, and the Dutch Second Reformation* (New York: Peter Lang, 1991).

For a persuasive apologetic that presents biblical Christianity as the only antidote for the modern drift towards skepticism, see J. Gresham Machen, *What is Faith?* (1925; reprint Grand Rapids: Eerdmans, 1962). Also helpful is Gordon Clark, *Faith and Saving Faith* (Jefferson, MD: Trinity, 1983).

Where should you begin? Consult the great Pauline chapters on faith, the classic Reformed doctrinal standards, and the major Reformed dogmatics. Then try Alexander Comrie, *The ABC of Faith*, translated by J. Marcus Banfield (Ossett, W. Yorks: Zoar, 1978). A Scots-turned-Dutch Second Reformation divine, Comrie (1706-1774) wrote extensively on the doctrine of saving faith and its relation to justification. In this work he explains the characteristics of saving faith by presenting twenty-eight scriptural words or phrases that describe the activity of faith (such as *coming, thirsting, believing, taking, committing*), and devoting a short chapter to each word.

ARTICLE 23

Justification

Happily, there is a rich supply of material on the doctrine of justification from a Protestant perspective. The seventeenth-century Reformed and Puritan divines have produced the best books on this critical "article by which the church stands or falls" (Luther). In addition to Reformed commentaries on Pauline epistles, Reformed confessional statements, and major Reformed dogmatics, consult the following:

Sixteenth and Seventeenth Centuries
Baxter, Richard. *A Treatise of Justifying Righteousness.* London: for N. Simmons and J. Robinson, 1676. The only unsound treatment on justification by a Puritan; neonomian in theology.
Brown, John (of Wamphray). *The Life of Justification Opened.* Edited by J. Koelman and M. Leydekker. Utrecht: n. p., 1695. Scarce, insightful.
Burgess, Anthony. *The True Doctrine of Iustification Asserted and Vindicated, From the Errors of Papists, Arminians, Socinians, and more especially Antinomians.* London: Robert White for Thomas Vnderhil, 1648. Thorough work by an able Puritan and Westminster Assembly divine. Soundly exegetical, experimental, and polemical.
Calvin, John. "Acts of the Council of Trent with the Antidote." In *Tracts and Treatises*, Vol. 3. Translated and edited by Henry Beveridge. Edinburgh: Calvin Translation Society, 1851; reprint Grand Rapids: Eerdmans, 1958, pp. 19-162. (Cf. Calvin's *Institutes*.)
Clarkson, David. "Justification by the Righteousness of Christ." In *The Works of David Clarkson.* Vol. 1, pp. 273-331. Edinburgh: Banner of Truth Trust, 1988. Brief Puritan treatment.

Davenant, John. *A Treatise on Justification, or the Disputatio de Justitia Habituali et Actuali*. Translated by Josiah Allport. 2 vols. London: Hamilton, Adams, & Co., 1844-46. Massive; shows strains of moderate Calvinism.

Downame, George. *A Treatise of Iustification*. London: Felix Kyngston for Nicolaus Bourne, 1633. Solid and savory Puritan work.

Eaton, John. *The Honey-combe of Free Justification by Christ Alone*. London: R. B. at the charge of R. Lancaster, 1642. Sound on justification, but contains hyper-Calvinistic tendencies.

Foxe, John. "Of Free Justification by Christ." In *Writings of John Fox, Bale, and Coverdale*. London: Religious Tract Society, 1831, pp. 131-286. Reveals that Foxe was more than a martyrologist.

Grew, Obadiah. *A Sinner's Justification, or the Lord Jesvs Christ the Lord our righteousnesse*. London: Printed for Nevil Simmons, 1670. Solid Puritan work.

Hooker, Thomas. *The soules Justification, on 2 Cor. 5:21*. London: Iohn Haviland, for Andrew Crooke, 1638. Experimental.

Traill, Robert. "A Vindication of the Protestant Doctrine Concerning Justification." In *The Works of Robert Traill*. Edinburgh: Banner of Truth Trust, 1986, Vol. 1, pp. 252-96. Defends Protestant doctrine from antinomian charges.

Nineteenth Century

Buchanan, James. *The Doctrine of Justification: An Outline of Its History in the Church and of Its Exposition from Scripture*. Edinburgh: T. & T. Clark, 1867; reprint Grand Rapids: Baker, 1977. Thoroughly grounded in the Scriptures; stresses the imputation of the righteousness of Christ to the believer.

Girardeau, John L. *Calvinism and Evangelical Arminianism: Compared as to Election, Reprobation, Justification, and Related Doctrines*. Columbia, 1890; reprint Harrisonburg, VA: Sprinkle, 1984. Capable work by a Southern Presbyterian theologian.

Halyburton, Thomas. "An Inquiry into the Nature of God's Act of Justification." In *The Works of Thomas Halyburton*. Edited by Robert Burns. Glasgow: Blackie & Son, 1837, pp. 559-67. The most helpful short treatment.

Hodge, Charles. *Justification by Faith Alone*. Reprint Hobbs, NM: Trinity Foundation, 1994. Hodge at his best.

Huntington, William. "The Justification of a Sinner and Satan's Lawsuit with Him." In *The Works of the Reverend William*

Huntington, Vol. 4. London: for E. Huntington by T. Bensley, 1833, pp. 3-285. Strikingly helpful in places, but leans in a hyper-Calvinistic direction.

Ritschl, Albrecht. *A Critical History of the Christian Doctrine of Justification and Reconciliation.* Translated by J. S. Black. Edinburgh: Edmonston and Douglas, 1872. Famous work by a German Protestant theologian, but denies the propitiatory character of Christ's death. Liberal and unsound.

Twentieth Century

Beeke, Joel R. *Justification by Faith: Selected Bibliography.* Grand Rapids: Reformation Heritage Books, 1995. Contains 550 bibliographical entries.

Berkouwer, Gerrit C. *Faith and Justification.* Translated by Lewis B. Smedes. Grand Rapids: Eerdmans, 1954. Helpful but ambiguous in places.

Boehl, Edward. *The Reformed Doctrine of Justification.* Translated by C. H. Riedesel. Reprint Grand Rapids: Eerdmans, 1946. Read Berkhof's enlightening introduction.

Carson, D. A., ed. *Right with God: Justification in the Bible and the World.* Grand Rapids: Baker, 1993. A real mix of essays, but overall insightful.

Gerstner, John H. *A Primer on Justification.* Phillipsburg, NJ: Presbyterian and Reformed, 1983. Basic, simple treatment.

MacArthur, John, R. C. Sproul, Joel Beeke, John Gerstner, John Armstrong. *Justification by Faith Alone: Affirming the doctrine by which the church and the individual stands or falls.* Morgan, PA: Soli Deo Gloria, 1995. Authors focus on Reformed understanding of each word in the phrase, "justification by faith alone."

Packer, James I., et al. *Here We Stand: Justification by Faith Today.* London: Hodder and Stoughton, 1986. Essays of mixed value.

Pink, Arthur W. *The Doctrines of Election and Justification.* Grand Rapids: Baker, 1974. Edifying.

Sproul, R.C. *Faith Alone: The Evangelical Doctrine of Justification.* Grand Rapids: Baker, 1995. Helpful; good place to start.

Toon, Peter. *Justification and Sanctification.* Westchester, IL: Crossway, 1983. Helpful treatment.

Historical Studies

Bennett, James. *Justification as Revealed in Scripture, in opposition to the*

Council of Trent, and Mr. Newman's Lectures. London: Hamilton, Adams, & Co., 1840.

Cunningham, William. "Justification." *Historical Theology.* Reprint London: Banner of Truth Trust, 1960, 2:1-120.

Duurschmidt, Kurt. "Some Aspects of Justification and Sanctification as seen in the Writings of some of the Magisterial and Radical Reformers." Ph.D. dissertation, Syracuse University, 1971.

Gore, Ralph J. "The Lutheran Ordo Salutis with Special Reference to Justification and Sanctification: A Reformed Analysis." Master's thesis, Faith Theological Seminary, 1983.

Green, Lowell C. *How Melanchthon Helped Luther Discover the Gospel: The Doctrine of Justification in the Reformation.* Fallbrook, CA: Verdict Publications, 1979.

Hagglund, Bengt. *The Background of Luther's Doctrine of Justification in Late Medieval Theology.* Philadelphia: Fortress Press, 1971.

Heinz, Johann. *Justification and Merit: Luther vs. Catholicism.* Berrien Springs, MI: Andrews University Press, 1981.

Leaver, Robin A. *The Doctrine of Justification in the Church of England.* Oxford: Latimer House, 1979.

_____. *Luther on Justification.* St. Louis: Concordia, 1975.

McGrath, Alister E. *Iustitia Dei: A History of the Doctrine of Justification.* 2 vols. Cambridge: Cambridge University Press, 1986.

Plantinga, Jacob. "The Time of Justification." Th.M. thesis, Westminster Theological Seminary, 1977.

Snell, Farley W. "The Place of Augustine in Calvin's Concept of Righteousness." Th.D. dissertation, Union Theological Seminary, 1968.

ARTICLE 24
Sanctification and Holiness

For the classic Reformed view of sanctification, holiness, and good works, one could do no better than read substantial portions of Book 3 of John Calvin's *Institutes of the Christian Religion* (Philadelphia: Westminster Press, 1960).

Whereas the Reformers excelled in the doctrine of justification, the Puritans were best on sanctification. Most frequently reprinted is Walter Marshall (1628-1680), *The Gospel Mystery of Sanctification* (1692; reprint Grand Rapids: Zondervan, 1954). Marshall effectively grounds the doctrine of sanctification in a believer's union with Christ and underscores the necessity of practical holiness in everyday living. By grace, he lived what he wrote. In the preface to his funeral sermon, Samuel Tomlyns says about his friend: "He wooed for Christ in his preaching, and allured you to Christ by his walking." Also stimulating is Thomas Brooks (1608-1680), "The Crown and Glory of Christianity: or Holiness, The only way to Happiness," in *The Works of Thomas Brooks* (1864; reprint Edinburgh: Banner of Truth Trust, 1980). It's a heart-searching, 450-page treatise on holiness which has been mysteriously neglected in contemporary studies. Richard Baxter (1615-1691), "The Spiritual and Carnal Man Compared and Contrasted; or, The Absolute Necessity and Excellency of Holiness," in *The Select Practical Works of Richard Baxter* (Glasgow: Blackie & Son, 1840), pp. 115-291, is similar to the writing of Brooks. But Baxter, though edifying in the area of sanctification, is not a reliable guide on justification.

An excellent eighteenth-century treatise on sanctification is James Fraser, *A Treatise on Sanctification* (1774; reprint Audubon, NJ: Old Paths, 1992).

The three best, nineteenth-century works on sanctification are: George Bethune, *The Fruit of the Spirit* (1839; reprint Swengel, PA:

Reiner, 1972), which is based on Galatians 5:22-23; Horatius Bonar, *God's Way of Holiness* (1869; reprint Pensacola, FL: Mt. Zion Publications, 1994), which is plain, packed, poignant, and powerful; J.C. Ryle, *Holiness: Its Nature, Hindrances, Difficulties, and Roots* (1879; reprint Greensboro, NC: Homiletic Press, 1956), which has long been regarded as a readable classic. Of Ryle's work, M. Lloyd-Jones wrote, "Ryle, like his great master, has no easy way to holiness to offer us, and no 'patent' method by which it can be obtained; but he invariably produces that 'hunger and thirst after righteousness' which is the only indispensable condition to being filled."

The last half of the twentieth century has produced a plethora of books on holiness. Noteworthy titles include Gerrit C. Berkouwer, *Faith and Sanctification*, translated by John Vriend (Grand Rapids: Eerdmans, 1952); A. W. Pink, *The Doctrine of Sanctification* (Swengel, PA: Bible Truth Depot, 1955); Stephen C. Neill, *Christian Holiness* (Guildford, England: Lutterworth, 1960); John W. Sanderson, *The Fruit of the Spirit* (Grand Rapids: Zondervan, 1972); Jay Adams, *Godliness Through Discipline* (Grand Rapids: Baker, 1973); Jerry Bridges, *The Pursuit of Holiness* and *The Practice of Holiness* (Colorado Springs: NavPress, 1978, 1983); Hugh D. Morgan, *The Holiness of God and of His People* (Bridgend, Wales: Evangelical Press of Wales, 1979); Kenneth Prior, *The Way of Holiness: A Study in Christian Growth* (Downers Grove, IL: InterVarsity Press, 1982); Peter Toon, *Justification and Sanctification* (Westchester, IL: Crossway, 1983); Roger Roberts, *Holiness: Every Christian's Calling* (Nashville: Broadman Press, 1985); Sinclair Ferguson, "The Reformed View," in *Christian Spirituality: Five Views of Sanctification*, edited by Donald L. Alexander (Downers Grove, IL: InterVarsity Press, 1988); James I. Packer, *Rediscovering Holiness* (Ann Arbor: Servant, 1992); Joel R. Beeke, *Holiness: God's Call to Sanctification* (Edinburgh: Banner of Truth Trust, 1994).

Where should you begin? Read Bonar, Ryle, Packer, Pink, and Marshall in that order.

ARTICLE 25
The Ceremonial Law

Sixteenth Century

The best work on the ceremonial law by a Reformer is *The Decades of Henry Bullinger*, translated by H.I. (1550 in Latin; Cambridge: University Press, 1850), Vol. 3, Sermon 6 ("Of the Ceremonial Law of God, but especially of the Priesthood, Time, and Place, Appointed for the Ceremonies," pp. 125-217) and Sermon 8 ("Of the Use or Effect of the Law of God, and of the Fulfilling and Abrogating of the Same: Of the Likeness and Difference of Both the Testaments and People, the Old and the New," pp. 236-300).

Seventeenth Century

For a balanced treatment on the ceremonial law from a great seventeenth-century theologian, see Francis Turretin, *Institutes of Elenctic Theology*, Vol. 2, translated by George Musgrave Giger, edited by James T. Dennison, Jr. (1683 in Latin; Philipsburg, NJ: P & R, 1994), Chaps. 24-25. Turretin answers these questions: "What was the end and use of the ceremonial law under the Old Testament? Was the ceremonial law abrogated under the New Testament? When and how?"

Eighteenth Century

Helpful eighteenth-century works on the ceremonial law include Wilhelmus à Brakel, *The Christian's Reasonable Service*, translated by Bartel Elshout, Vol. 4 (1700 in Dutch; Morgan, PA: Soli Deo Gloria, 1995), pp. 421-502; Herman Witsius, *The Economy of the Covenants Between God and Man*, translated by William Crookshank, Vol. 2 (1772; reprint Escondido, CA: Den Dulk Foundation, 1990), Chaps. 9-14; John Brown of Haddington, *An*

Introduction to the Right Understanding of the Oracles of God (Albany: Barber & Southwick, 1793), Chap. 3 on "Jewish Laws and Types."

Nineteenth Century

There is a plethora of nineteenth-century works on the tabernacle and temple. Among the best are Henry W. Soltau, *The Holy Vessels and Furniture of the Tabernacle* (1851; reprint Grand Rapids: Kregel, 1974) and *The Tabernacle, The Priesthood, and the Offerings* (1857; reprint Grand Rapids: Kregel 1972); Alfred Edersheim, *The Temple: Its Ministry and Services* (1874; reprint Grand Rapids: Eerdmans, 1958); Dirk H. Dolman and Marcus Rainsford, *The Tabernacle*, 2 vols. in 1 (reprint Minneapolis: Klock & Klock, 1982).

Standard conservative works of the past century that contain substantial sections on ceremonial law include Patrick Fairbairn, *The Typology of Scripture*, 2 vols. (1845; reprint Grand Rapids: Baker, 1975) and *The Revelation of Law in Scripture* (1869; reprint Grand Rapids: Zondervan, 1957); J. H. Kurtz, *Sacrificial Worship of the Old Testament*, translated by James Martin (1863; Grand Rapids: Baker, 1980); Ernst W. Hengstenberg, *History of the Kingdom of God Under the Old Testament*, translated by Theodore Meyer and James Martin, 2 vols. (1871-72; reprint Grand Rapids: Kregel, 1975). Gustav Friedrich Oehler, *Theology of the Old Testament*, translated by Ellen D. Smith and Sophia Taylor, revised by George E. Day (1883; reprint Grand Rapids: Zondervan, n.d.), pp. 246-352, is generally sound but occasionally lapses into rationalism.

Twentieth Century

For this century, the primary conservative works on Old Testament theology that elaborate on the ceremonial law include John Howard Raven, *The History of the Religion of Israel: An Old Testament Theology* (1933; reprint Grand Rapids: Baker, 1979), pp. 42-155; Geerhardus Vos, *Biblical Theology* (1948; reprint Grand Rapids: Eerdmans, 1975), pp. 143-82; J. Barton Payne, *The Theology of the Older Testament* (Grand Rapids: Zondervan, 1962).

See Vern Poythress, *The Shadow of Christ in the Law of Moses* (Brentwood, TN: Wolgemuth & Hyatt, 1991) for some fresh thinking on the ceremonial law and for an excellent bibliography. For a helpful analysis of the state of the field and an extensive bibliography in Old Testament theology, see Gerhard F. Hasel, *Old*

Testament Theology: Basic Issues in the Current Debate, rev. ed. (Grand Rapids: Eerdmans, 1991).

Where should you begin? Read Turretin for an introduction to the subject, then turn to à Brakel, Vos, and Poythress. But don't neglect Bullinger, if you can obtain a copy.

ARTICLE 26
Christ's Intercession

Christ's intercession is a comfort for believers and ought to be the endearing subject of many treatises. Surprisingly, few good works have been written from a Reformed perspective on the intercession of our Lord at the Father's right hand.

For pre-eighteenth-century material, consult the various Reformed confessions and Reformed dogmatics (cf. *Reformed Dogmatics Set Out and Illustrated from the Sources*, edited by H. Heppe, translated by G. T. Thomson [Grand Rapids: Zondervan, 1978]).

For an eighteenth-century work that includes a substantial portion on Christ's intercession, see John Hurrion, *The Knowledge of Christ Glorified, Opened and Applied in Twelve Sermons on Christ's Resurrection, Ascension, Sitting at God's Right Hand, Intercession and Judging the World* (London: Clark and Hett, 1729). This scarce book is a gold mine of scriptural, experimental truth displaying the riches of Christ in a series of sermons preached in 1700.

The two best, nineteenth-century treatises on Christ's intercession are William Symington, *On the Atonement and Intercession of Jesus Christ* (New York: Robert Carter, 1863) and William Milligan, *The Ascension and Heavenly Priesthood of Our Lord* (Edinburgh: T. & T. Clark, 1891). In a succinct, 50-page treatment, Symington covers the reality, nature, matter, properties, and results of Christ's intercession. Milligan's book, the Baird lectures for 1891, focuses on Christ's post-resurrection ministry on earth and His present ministry in heaven. Though Milligan is often underrated as a writer, he is full of valuable, scriptural substance.

The best twentieth-century work is Henry H. Meeter, *The Heavenly High Priesthood of Christ: An Exegetico-Dogmatic Study* (Grand Rapids: Eerdmans-Sevensma, 1916). Chapters 12 and 13 masterfully cover the intercession and benediction of our heavenly

High Priest. Henry B. Swete, *The Ascended Christ: A Study in the Earliest Christian Teaching* (London: Macmillan, 1913) stresses Christ's role as intercessor and advocate. Peter Toon, *The Ascension of Our Lord* (Nashville: Thomas Nelson, 1984) explores all aspects of Christ's ascension: its foreshadowing in the Old Testament, accounts of it in the New, and the teaching of the church through the ages.

For helpful works on our Lord's intercession in John 17, read Thomas Manton, "Sermons Upon the Seventeenth Chapter of St. John," in *The Complete Works of Thomas Manton*, (London: Nisbet, 1872), 10:109-490; 11:1-149; Charles Ross, *The Inner Sanctuary* (1888; reprint London: Banner of Truth Trust, 1967), pp. 199-247; H. C. G. Moule, *The High Priestly Prayer: A Devotional Commentary on the Seventeenth Chapter of John* (1907; reprint Grand Rapids: Baker, 1978); Marcus Rainsford, *Our Lord Prays for His Own: Thoughts on John 17* (Chicago: Moody Press, 1950); four volumes of Martyn Lloyd-Jones on John 17, *Studies in Jesus' Prayer for His Own* (Westchester, IL: Crossway, 1988-89).

For a historical-theological study, see W. H. Marravee, *The Ascension of Christ in the Works of St. Augustine* (Ottawa: University of Ottawa Press, 1967).

ARTICLE 27

The Doctrine of the Church

Sixteenth Century
Calvin's *Institutes*, Book 4, Chapter 1, "The True Church with Which as Mother of All the Godly We Must Keep Unity," presents the basics of Reformed ecclesiology (Battles edition, 2:1011-1040). The first four sermons of Volume 5 of Henry Bullinger's *Decades*, translated by H. I. (Cambridge: University Press, 1852), pp. 1-163, are more pervasive and helpful than Calvin, particularly in dealing with the attributes and unity of the church.

Eighteenth Century
Wilhelmus à Brakel, *The Christian's Reasonable Service*, translated by Bartel Elshout (Ligonier, PA: Soli Deo Gloria, 1993), 2:3-187, is an early eighteenth-century work that covers ecclesiology in nearly the same order as the Belgic Confession.

Nineteenth Century
James Bannerman, *The Church of Christ*, 2 vols. (1869; reprint London: Banner of Truth Trust, 1960) is the most extensive (950 pages), standard, Reformed treatment of the doctrine of the church. The Banner edition supplies an able biographical introduction on Cunningham and Bannerman by Iain Murray. Subtitled *A Treatise on The Nature, Powers, Ordinances, Discipline, and Government of the Christian Church*, Bannerman's *magnum opus* remains the classic Reformed work on ecclesiology.

The volumes of James Bannerman are edited and prefaced by Douglas Bannerman, who has also written an able 590-page treatise, *The Scripture Doctrine of the Church Historically and Exegetically Considered* (1887; reprint Grand Rapids: Eerdmans, 1955), covering the development of the church from the time of Abraham through the ministry of Paul.

Charles Hodge, *Church and Its Polity* (London: Nelson and Sons, 1879) is a masterful presentation of Reformed ecclesiology in addition to the treatment of this subject in his systematic theology.

Twentieth Century

R. B. Kuiper, *The Glorious Body of Christ: A Scriptural Appreciation of the One Holy Church* (Grand Rapids: Eerdmans, 1955) is the most basic, poignant Reformed treatment of the doctrine of the church in English. It is a wide-ranging volume, covering more than fifty topics in short, edifying chapters, including the church's unity, marks, offices, responsibilities, privileges, and relationship to the world. Kuiper is vigorous, clear, and comprehensive.

G. C. Berkouwer, *The Church*, translated by James E. Davison (Grand Rapids: Eerdmans, 1976) emphasizes the unity, catholicity, apostolicity, and holiness of the church as it expounds its true ministry. Indecisive and provocative in places, it is enlightening and edifying elsewhere.

Edmund Clowney, former president of Westminster Theological Seminary (Philadelphia), has written cogently and extensively on the Reformed doctrine of the church. For a succinct exposition, see *The Doctrine of the Church* (Philadelphia: Presbyterian and Reformed, 1976); for a more in-depth treatment reflecting the author's mature thought, read *The Church* (Downers Grove, IL: InterVarsity Press, 1996).

Historical-Theological Studies

Thomas M. Lindsay, *The Church and the Ministry in the Early Centuries* (1910; reprint Minneapolis: James Family, 1977) details how the image of the church, its officers, and its ministry changed after the completion of the New Testament. It proficiently covers events from the New Testament to the fourth century.

For a scholarly treatment of the views of the Reformers on ecclesiology, with a special focus on Luther, see Paul D. L. Avis, *The Church in the Theology of the Reformers* (Atlanta: Knox Press, 1981). Unfortunately, Avis's personal development of an ecclesiology based on Luther's views is unscriptural and stained with liberalism. For Calvin's views, see *John Calvin and the Church*, edited by Timothy George (Louisville: Westminster/John Knox Press, 1990), especially Part 3, which shows how Calvin serves as a centering focus of various issues that touch on the life of the church.

For an extensive bibliography on ecclesiology that can provide assistance despite its Roman Catholic orientation, see A. Dulles and P. Granfield, *The Church: A Bibliography* (Wilmington: Glazier, 1985).

Where should you begin reading? Definitely with R.B. Kuiper, then Calvin and à Brakel. Then you will be ready to study James Bannerman.

ARTICLE 28
Church Membership

The best brief treatment on church membership is Wilhelmus à Brakel, "The Duty to Join the Church and to Remain with Her," in *The Christian's Reasonable Service*, translated by Bartel Elshout (Ligonier, PA: Soli Deo Gloria, 1993), 2:55-86. à Brakel takes seriously the commitment of church membership and warns earnestly against the dangers of schism.

Books that explain the questions publicly confessed in the Dutch Reformed tradition include Nicholas J. Monsma, *This I Confess: Being a brief Explanation of the Form for the Public Profession of Faith* (Holland, MI: n.p., 1936); John D. Hellinga and Harry VanDyken, *"Do You Heartily Believe...?" A Preparation Manual for Public Confession of Faith* (n.p., n.d.).

Works of varying merit on how to practice the obligations of church membership include the following: John Angell James, *Christian Fellowship, Or the Church Member's Guide*, edited by J. O. Choules (Boston: Lincoln & Edmands, 1829), which includes excellent chapters on the purpose and privileges of church membership, the duties of church members in relationship to themselves, to each other, to their pastor, to other Christian organizations, and to their own unique personalities and callings; William Crowell, *The Church Member's Manual* (Boston: Gould, Kendall, & Lincoln, 1847), subtitled *Ecclesiastical Principles, Doctrine, and Discipline: Presenting a Systematic View of the Structure, Polity, Doctrines, and Practices of Christian Churches, as Taught in the Scriptures*; Jan Karel VanBaalen, *If Thou Shalt Confess* (Grand Rapids: Eerdmans, 1927), which covers believing and confessing, reading, teaching, social life, tithing, temptations, prayer, trials, recreation, the Lord's Day, and serving others; Abraham Kuyper, *The Implications of Public Confession*, translated by Henry Zylstra (Grand Rapids:

Zondervan, 1934), which addresses a variety of subjects such as prayer, communion with other believers, practicing good stewardship, and participating in the life of the church; L. H. VanDer Meiden, *God's Yea and Your Amen*, translated by Cornelius Lambregtse (Grand Rapids: Board of Publications of the Old Christian Reformed Church, 1972), which focuses especially on the sacraments in relation to public profession of faith; J. Geertsema, W. Huizinga, A.B. Roukema, G. VanDooren, W.W.J. VanOene, *Before Many Witnesses* (Winnipeg: Premier, 1974), which explains what public profession means and examines a member's obligation to serve others within and outside of the body of Christ; A. Hoogerland, *Making Confession and Then...?*, translated by Garret J. Moerdyk (Grand Rapids: Eerdmans, 1984), which relates confession of faith to parents, walk of life, dress, the Lord's Supper, the Lord's Day, the covenant of grace, church offices, marriage, reading material, and death.

For a confession-of-faith course, see Joel R. and James W. Beeke, *Bible Doctrine Student Workbook: An Introductory Course* (Grand Rapids: Eerdmans, 1982), which contains 568 questions for confession-of-faith class attendees and covers the basics of Reformed doctrine, including the commitments and implications involved in full, professing church membership. An accompanying *Teacher's Guide,* which provides answers to all the questions, is available upon request.

ARTICLE 29

The True and the False Church Compared

For a condensed treatment, see John Calvin, *Institutes of the Christian Religion* (Philadelphia: Westminster Press, 1960), pp. 1041-1052 (Book 4, Chapter 2). Calvin's focus here is on the false church; he argues that departure from true doctrine and worship invalidates the Roman Catholic Church's claim to be the true church. For a somewhat fuller explanation, read Wilhelmus à Brakel, *The Christian's Reasonable Service,* translated by Bartel Elshout (Ligonier, PA: Soli Deo Gloria, 1993), 2:15-54. à Brakel excels in explaining the distinguishing marks of the true church; that the true church is separated from the world and united internally, confesses Christ and His truth, engages in spiritual warfare, and glorifies God. He also makes a formidable case from Scripture for linking the Antichrist with the papacy (pp. 44-53).

For works exposing the fallacies of the Roman Catholic Church, see Loraine Boettner, *Roman Catholicism* (London: Banner of Truth Trust, 1966), which is a basic yet perceptive evaluation, that exposes the false teachings of the Roman Catholic Church; J. B. Rowell, *Papal Infallibility* (Grand Rapids: Kregel, 1970), which examines the foundations and claims on which the Roman Catholic church is founded. Two of the most helpful contemporary authors who provide considerable assistance in exposing Roman Catholic theology for what it is are William Webster (*Salvation: The Bible and Roman Catholicism* [Edinburgh: Banner of Truth Trust, 1990]; *The Church of Rome at the Bar of History* [Edinburgh: Banner of Truth Trust, 1995]) and John Armstrong (ed., *Roman Catholicism: Evangelical Protestants Analyze What Divides and Unites Us* [Chicago: Moody, 1994] and *A View of Rome* [Chicago: Moody, 1995]). The infamous statement, titled *Evangelicals and Catholics Together (ECT)* released in March 1994, has evoked a number of reactions, including John Ankerberg and John Weldon, *Protestants and Catholics: Do They Now Agree?* (Eugene, OR: Harvest House, 1995); Kevin Reed, *Making Shipwreck of the Faith* (Dallas: Protestant Heritage, 1995). ECT has also prompted a trio of books edited by Don Kistler and published by Soli Deo Gloria, each of which affirms historic Protestant doctrine: *Justification by Faith Alone* (1995); *Sola Scriptura! The Protestant Position on the Bible* (1996); *Trust and Obey* (1997).

For guidance on how to deal with scandal and heresy in the church, read John Calvin, *Concerning Scandals,* translated by John W. Fraser (Grand Rapids: Eerdmans, 1978). It covers intrinsic and extrinsic scandals, as well as "troubles of various kinds." Calvin is profitable, as usual, but no work has superseded that of James Durham, *The Dying Man's Testament to the Church of Scotland or, A Treatise Concerning Scandal,* edited by Christopher Coldwell (Dallas, TX: Naphtali Press, 1990). First published in 1680, this classic has finally been properly edited and freshly printed. After introducing the subject of scandals in general, Durham ably addresses public scandals, doctrinal scandals, and scandalous divisions. His work concludes with how to foster genuine unity in the church. J.C. Ryle, *Warnings to the Churches* (London: Banner of Truth Trust, 1967), first published in 1877 as part of *Knots Untied,* deals with various dangers facing the church and how we ought to respond to them.

ARTICLE 30

Church Government and Offices

Two helpful works advocating Presbyterian church government were written in 1646 while the Westminster Assembly was in session. *Jus Divinum Regiminis Ecclesiastici or The Divine Right of Church Government, originally asserted and evidenced by the Holy Scriptures by the Ministers of Sion College, London, December 1646* (Dallas: Naphtali Press, 1995) contains an able introduction by David Hall on the Westminster Assembly's original intent in church government as clarified by this work. Samuel Rutherford, *The Divine Right of Church Government and Excommunication* (London: Iohn Field for Christopher Meredith), is quite polemical but touches on a number of church-government issues that are still debated today.

Helpful nineteenth-century works on church government include John Brown (of Gartmore), *Vindication of the Presbyterian Form of Church Government* (Edinburgh: H. Inglis, 1805); Samuel Miller, *Presbyteriansim the Truly Primitive and Apostolical Constitution of the Church of Christ* (Philadelphia: Presbyterian Board of Publication, 1835); R. J. Breckinridge, *Presbyterian Government*, edited with helpful introductory essay by Kevin Reed (Dallas: Presbyterian Heritage, 1988) — extracted from Breckinridge's major work, *Presbyterian Government, Not a Hierarchy, But a Commonwealth: and, Presbyterian Ordination, Not a Charm, But an Act of Government*, which was originally published in 1843 as a supplement to *The Spirit of the XIX Century*; William Cunningham, *Discussions on Church Principles: Popish, Erastian, and Presbyterian* (1863; reprint Edmonton: Still Waters Revival Books, 1991), as well as Cunningham's chapter on church government in *Historical Theology* (1862; reprint Edinburgh: Banner of Truth Trust, 1979), 2:514-56.

For a newer, helpful booklet on church government, read Kevin

Reed, *Biblical Church Government* (Dallas: Presbyterian Heritage, 1983). For how government ought to be exercised by church office-bearers, a recent volume edited by Mark R. Brown is most helpful. *Order in the Offices: Essays Defining the Roles of Church Officers* (Duncansville, PA: Classic Presbyterians Government Resources, 1993) contains fifteen essays (Charles Hodge, Edmund Clowney, Iain Murray, Leonard Coppes, Robert Rayburn, Charles Dennison, etc.) that help foster "peace and order in the church, as the roles and relationships of ministers, elders, and deacons are clarified." It includes an excellent, annotated bibliography.

Where should you begin? For church government, study Reed; for church offices, read Brown.

ARTICLE 31

Ministers, Elders, and Deacons

Ministers

Solomon's adage, "Of making many books there is no end," certainly applies to the office of the ministry. Some of the best works on homiletics (i.e., preaching) are: William Perkins, *The Art of Prophesying with The Calling of the Ministry* (1605-1606; reprint Edinburgh: Banner of Truth Trust, 1996); Philip Doddridge, *Lectures on Preaching* (London: Richard Edwards, 1804); Gardiner Spring, *The Power of the Pulpit* (1848; reprint Edinburgh: Banner of Truth Trust, 1986); John Claude, *An Essay on the Composition of a Sermon,* edited by Charles Simeon (New York: Carlton & Phillips, 1853); James W. Alexander, *Thoughts on Preaching* (1864; reprint Edinburgh: Banner of Truth Trust, 1975); Robert L. Dabney, *Sacred Rhetoric or A Course of Lectures on Preaching* (1870; reprint Edinburgh: Banner of Truth Trust, 1979); John A. Broadus, *On the Preparation and Delivery of Sermons,* 4th ed. (1870; reprint New York: Harper & Row, 1979); M. Reu, *Homiletics: A Manual of The Theory and Practice of Preaching,* translated by Albert Steinhaeuser (Chicago: Wartburg, 1924); Albert N. Martin, *What's Wrong with Preaching Today?* (London: Banner of Truth Trust, 1967); D. Martyn Lloyd-Jones, *Preaching and Preachers* (Grand Rapids: Zondervan, 1971); Homer C. Hoeksema, "Homiletics" (Grandville, MI: Protestant Reformed Theological Seminary, 1975); Pierre Charles Marcel, *The Relevance of Preaching,* translated by R. R. McGregor (Grand Rapids: Baker, 1977); John R. W. Stott, *Between Two Worlds: The Art of Preaching in the Twentieth Century* (Grand Rapids: Eerdmans, 1982); Samuel T. Logan, Jr., ed., *The Preacher and Preaching: Reviving the Art in the Twentieth Century* (Philipsburg, NJ: Presbyterian and Reformed, 1986); John MacArthur, Jr., et al., *Rediscovering Expository Preaching* (Dallas: Word, 1992).

Significant works on pastoral theology (i.e., the minister's personal life, pastoral duties, and preaching) include: Richard Baxter, *The Reformed Pastor* (1656; unabridged reprint New York: Robert Carter, 1860); Herman Witsius, *On the Character of a True Theologian,* edited by J. Ligon Duncan III (1675; reprint Greenville, SC: Reformed Academic Press, 1994); Samuel Bownas, *A Description of the Qualifications Necessary to A Gospel Minister* (London: Luke Hinde, 1750); John Mason, *The Student and Pastor* (London: H. D. Symonds, 1807); John Brown, ed., *The Christian Pastor's Manual* (1826; reprint Ligonier: Soli Deo Gloria, 1991); Charles Bridges, *The Christian Ministry* (1830; reprint London: Banner of Truth Trust, 1959); John Angell James, *An Earnest Ministry: The Want of the Times* (1847; reprint Edinburgh: Banner of Truth Trust, 1993); Samuel Miller, *Letters on Clerical Manners and Habits* (Philadelphia: Presbyterian Board of Publication, 1852); A. Vinet, *Pastoral Theology,* translated by Thomas H. Skinner (New York: Ivison & Phinney, 1854); William G.T. Shedd, *Homiletics and Pastoral Theology* (1867; reprint London: Banner of Truth Trust, 1965); Patrick Fairbairn, *Pastoral Theology* (1875; reprint Audubon, NJ: Old Paths, 1992); William M. Taylor, *The Ministry of the Word* (1876; reprint Grand Rapids: Baker, 1975); Thomas Murphy, *Pastoral Theology* (1877; reprint Audubon, NJ: Old Paths, 1996); J. J. VanOosterzee, *Practical Theology: A Manual for Theological Students,* translated by Maurice J. Evans (London: Hodder and Stoughton, 1878); Charles H. Spurgeon, *Lectures to My Students* (1881; reprint Pasadena, TX: Pilgrim, 1990); George Campbell Morgan, *The Ministry of the Word* (1919; reprint Grand Rapids: Baker, 1970); Homer A. Kent, Sr., *The Pastor and His Work* (Chicago: Moody, 1963); Ralph G. Turnbull, ed., *Baker's Dictionary of Practical Theology* (Grand Rapids: Baker, 1967).

For historical studies on preaching, see John Ker, *Lectures on the History of Preaching* (New York: A.C. Armstrong & Son, 1893); Charles Smyth, *The Art of Preaching: A Practical Survey of Preaching in the Church of England, 737-1939* (London: SPCK, 1940); Hugh Thomson Kerr, *Preaching in the Early Church* (New York: Fleming H. Revell, 1942); Edwin Charles Dargan and Ralph G. Turnbull, *A History of Preaching,* 3 vols. (reprint Grand Rapids: Baker, 1974).

Elders

Helpful books on the eldership include: John Glass, "Of the Unity and Distinction of the Elder's Office," in *Works of John Glass,*

Vol. 2 (Perth, 1782); Samuel Miller, *An Essay on the Warrant, Nature and Duties of the Ruling Elder* (1832; reprint Dallas: Presbyterian Heritage, 1987); Thomas Smyth, *The Name, Nature, and Functions of Ruling Elders* (1845; reprint Duncansville, PA: Classic Presbyterians Government Resources, 1992) — best read in conjunction with his two later sets of journal articles, "Theories of the Eldership," in *Complete Works of Rev. Thomas Smyth*, 4:167-275, 277-358; Peter Colin Campbell, *The Theory of Ruling Eldership* (1866; reprint Duncansville, PA: Classic Presbyterian Government Resources, 1992); David Dickson, *The Elder and His Work* (1875; reprint Dallas: Presbyterian Heritage, 1990); J. Aspinwall Hodge, *The Ruling Elder at Work* (Philadelphia: Presbyterian Board of Publication, 1901); William Henry Roberts, *Manual for Ruling Elders* (Philadelphia: Presbyterian Board of Publication, 1905); T. Graham Campbell, *The Work of the Eldership* (Glasgow: John Smith & Son, 1915); Cleland Boyd McAfee, *The Ruling Elder* (Philadelphia: Presbyterian Board of Christian Education, 1931); G. D. Henderson, *The Scottish Ruling Elder* (London: James Clark, 1935); Robert W. Henderson, *Profiles of the Eldership: 1974* (Geneva: WARC, 1975); Lawrence R. Eyres, *The Elders of the Church* (Philadelphia: Presbyterian and Reformed, 1975); Gerard Berghoef and Lester DeKoster, *The Elders Handbook: A Practical Guide for Church Leaders* (Grand Rapids: Christian's Library Press, 1979), with a companion study guide published in 1994; Paul S. Wright, *The Presbyterian Elder* (Philadelphia: Westminster, 1986); Elsie Anne McKee, *Elders and the Plural Ministry* (Geneva: Librairie Droz, 1988); Alexander Strauch, *Biblical Eldership: An Urgent Call to Restore Biblical Church Leadership* (Littleton, CO: Lewis and Roth, 1988); John R. Sittema, *With a Shepherd's Heart: Reclaiming the Pastoral Office of Elder* (Grandville, MI: Reformed Fellowship, 1996).

For enlightening articles on the nature and validity of the office of elders, start with Iain Murray's "Ruling Elders — A Sketch of a Controversy," *Banner of Truth* No. 235 (April 1983): 1-9, and "The Problem of the 'Eldership' and Its Wider Implications," *Banner of Truth* No. 395-96 (Aug-Sep 1996):36-56. See also R.E.H. Uprichard, "The Eldership in Martin Bucer and John Calvin," *Evangelical Quarterly* 61:1 (1989):21-37. Uprichard aims to prove that Calvin rediscovered rather than invented the eldership (contra

T.F. Torrance, *The Eldership in the Reformed Church* [Edinburgh: Handsel Press, 1984]).

Deacons

Helpful works on the diaconate include William Guthrie, "A Treatise of Ruling Elders and Deacons," in *The Works of William Guthrie* (Glasgow, 1771); Peter Y. DeJong, *The Ministry of Mercy for Today* (Grand Rapids: Baker, 1968); Leonard J. Coppes, *Who Will Lead Us: A Study in the Development of Biblical Offices with Emphasis on the Diaconate* (Philipsburg, NJ: Pilgrim, 1977); Andrew Jumper, *Chosen to Serve: The Deacon* (Atlanta: John Knox Press, 1977); Gerard Berghoef and Lester DeKoster, *The Deacons Handbook: A Manual of Stewardship* (Grand Rapids: Christian's Library Press, 1980), with a companion study guide published in 1994.

ARTICLE 32
Church Order, Worship, and Discipline

Church Order

The best overall work on Reformed church order is edited by David W. Hall and Joseph H. Hall, *Paradigms in Polity: Classic Readings in Reformed and Presbyterian Church Government* (Grand Rapids: Eerdmans, 1994). This work also contains an outstanding bibliographical essay (pp. 603-616). Other generally helpful works include Charles Hodge, *Discussions in Church Polity* (New York: Charles Scribner's Sons, 1878) and J. L. Schaver, *The Polity of the Churches,* 2 vols. (Chicago: Church Polity Press, 1937). Schaver is oriented to the polity of the Christian Reformed Churches.

The famous Church Order of Dort (1619) is expounded most ably by Dutch church order experts such as H. Bouwman, F.L. Rutgers, and J. Janssen. English works rely heavily on those Dutch scholars. The most helpful work in English is Idzerd Van Dellen and Martin Monsma, *The Church Order Commentary* (Grand Rapids: Zondervan, 1941), which expounds the old Christian Reformed version of the Church Order of Dort. After the Christian Reformed Church adopted extensive revisions to their church order in 1965, Martin Monsma revised this useful work and published it under the same authorship as *The Revised Church Order Commentary* (Grand Rapids: Zondervan, 1967). Additional sources on the Church Order of Dort or denominational versions of it include: J. L. Schaver, *Christian Reformed Church Order* (Grand Rapids: Zondervan, 1937); Howard B. Spaan, *Christian Reformed Church Government* (Grand Rapids: Kregel, 1968); Herman Hanko, "Notes on the Church Order" (Grand Rapids: Theological School of the Protestant Reformed Churches, 1973); K. DeGier, *Explanation of the Church Order of Dordt in Questions and Answers,* edited by Joel Beeke (Grand Rapids: Eerdmans, 1980); G. VanRongen and K. Deddens,

Decently and in Good Order: the Church Order of the Canadian and American Reformed Churches (Winnipeg: Premier, 1986); W.W.J. VanOene, *With Common Consent: A practical guide to the use of the Church Order of the Canadian Reformed Churches* (Winnipeg: Premier, 1990).

Richard DeRidder has produced two helpful manuscripts that, unfortunately, remain unpublished: "A Survey of the Sources of Reformed Church Polity" (Grand Rapids: Calvin Theological Seminary, 1983), and "The Church Orders of the Sixteenth Century Reformed Churches of the Netherlands Together With Their Social, Political, and Ecclesiastical Context" (Grand Rapids: Calvin Theological Seminary, 1987). This latter manuscript is a massive work of 660 pages that contains full translations of all the articles of the major synods held in the Netherlands from 1568 to 1638.

For church polity of the New Testament, Samuel Davidson, *The Ecclesiastical Polity of the New Testament Unfolded* (London: Jackson and Walford, 1848) is more conservative than Eduard Schweizer, *Church Order in the New Testament* (London: SCM, 1961).

Worship and Liturgy

For Reformed worship and liturgy, see William Ames, *A Fresh Suit Against Human Ceremonies in God's Worship* (1633; photocopy format, Edmonton: Still Waters Revival Books, 1996); *The Directory for the Public Worship of God; agreed upon by the Assembly of Divines at Westminster* (1645); Jeremiah Burroughs, *Gospel Worship* (1646; reprint Morgan, PA: Soli Deo Gloria, 1990); Howard Hageman, *Pulpit and Table* (Richmond: Knox, 1962); James Hastings Nichols, *Corporate Worship in the Reformed Tradition* (Philadelphia; Westminster Press, 1968); G. VanDoren, *The Beauty of Reformed Liturgy* (Winnipeg: Premier, 1980); *Liturgy of the Reformed Churches* (1767 version used by the RCA; 1914 version printed with *The Psalter*; 1934 version printed with the *Psalter Hymnal*; 1991 version, which includes entire Dutch Reformed liturgy, printed as *The Doctrinal Standards, Liturgy and Church Order*); David Lachman and Frank J. Smith, eds., *Worship in the Presence of God* (Greenville, SC: Greenville Seminary Press, 1992); Arthur Pontier, "Call to Greatness: A Theology of Worship" (unpublished, 1994); Kevin Reed, *Biblical Worship* (Dallas: Presbyterian Heritage, 1995).

For historical-theological material on worship and liturgy, see especially Horton Davies, *Worship and Theology in England, 1534-1965*, 5 vols. (Princeton: University Press, 1961-75), as well as, *The Worship of the English Puritans* (Westminster: Dacre Press, 1948) and *The Worship of the American Puritans (1629-1730)* (New York: Peter Lang, 1990). Also see Charles Baird, *A Chapter on Liturgies: Historical Sketches* (London: Knight & Son, 1856); Bard Thompson, *Liturgies of the Western Church* (New York: Collins, 1962); Hughes Oliphant Old, *The Patristic Roots of Reformed Worship* (Zurich: Juris Druck, 1975); James F. White, *Protestant Worship: Traditions in Transition* (Louisville: Westminster/John Knox, 1989); John Harper, *The Forms and Orders of Western Liturgy from the Tenth to the Eighteenth Century* (Oxford: Clarendon Press, 1991); Paul Bradshaw, *The Search for the Origins of Christian Worship: Sources and Methods for the Study of Early Liturgy* (New York: Oxford, 1992); D. A. Carson, ed., *Worship: Adoration and Action* (Grand Rapids: Baker, 1993); James F. White, *A Brief History of Christian Worship* (Nashville: Abingdon, 1993).

Church Discipline

There is little good Reformed material on church discipline. The best work is Jay E. Adams, *Handbook of Church Discipline* (Grand Rapids: Zondervan, 1986). Also see Warham Walker, *Harmony in the Church: Church Discipline* (1844; reprint Rochester, NY: Backus, 1981); John White and Ken Blue, *Church Discipline that Heals* (Downers Grove, IL: InterVarsity Press, 1985); John Calvin, *Calvin's Ecclesiastical Advice,* translated by Mary Beaty and Benjamin W. Farley (Louisville, KY: Westminster/John Knox, 1991).

ARTICLE 33

The Sacraments

Though numerous, sound Reformed treatises expound baptism or the Lord's Supper, few treat both sacraments under one cover. Two of the best, succinct works are Ezekiel Hopkins, "The Doctrine of the Two Sacraments," in *The Works of Ezekiel Hopkins,* Vol. 2 (1867; reprint Morgan, PA: Soli Deo Gloria, 1997), pp. 301-359, and James S. Candlish, *The Christian Sacraments* (Edinburgh: T & T Clark, 1857). Stephen H. Tyng, *Fellowship with Christ: A Guide to the Sacraments* (New York: Protestant Episcopal Society for the Promotion of Evangelical Knowledge, 1854) is instructive and edifying. More detailed but not always as reliable are John S. Stone, *The Christian Sacraments* (New York: Anson D.F. Randolph, 1866), and Gerrit C. Berkouwer, *The Sacraments,* translated by Hugo Bekker (Grand Rapids: Eerdmans, 1969). Berkouwer provides an able critique of the teaching of Romanism and Lutheranism as well as various contemporary views of the sacraments.

Some of the best treatments of both sacraments from a Reformed perspective are buried in systematic theologies or sermon books, such as John Calvin, *Institutes of the Christian Religion* (Philadelphia: Westminster Press, 1960), 2:1276-1484; Henry Bullinger, *The Decades,* translated by H.I. (Cambridge: University Press, 1852), 4:226-351; Wilhelmus à Brakel, *The Christian's Reasonable Service,* translated by Bartel Elshout (Ligonier, PA: Soli Deo Gloria, 1993), 2:469-600. Also consult expositions of Lord's Days 25-30 of the Heidelberg Catechism, such as Herman Hoeksema, *The Triple Knowledge,* Vol. 2 (Grand Rapids: Reformed Free Pub. Assn., 1972).

For historical-theological works on the sacraments, see Ronald S. Wallace, *Calvin's Doctrine of the Word and Sacrament* (London: Oliver and Boyd, 1953); Joseph C. McLelland, *The Visible Words of God: An Exposition of the Sacramental Theology of Peter Martyr Vermigli,*

1500-1562 (Grand Rapids: Eerdmans, 1957); Robert S. Paul, *The Atonement and the Sacraments* (London: Hodder and Stoughton, 1960); E.B. Holifield, *The Covenant Sealed: The Development of Puritan Sacramental Theology in Old and New England, 1570-1720* (New Haven: Yale University Press, 1974).

ARTICLE 34

Holy Baptism

Some of the best works on the doctrine of holy baptism include:

Eighteenth Century

William Wall, *The History of Infant Baptism* (London: Joseph Downing, 1707); William Wall, *A Defence of the History of Infant Baptism Against the Reflections of Mr. Gale and Others* (London: R. Bonwicke, et al., 1720); Samuel Clarke, *Three Practical Essays on Baptism, Confirmation and Repentance* (London: John and Paul Knapton, 1740).

Nineteenth Century

John Hubbard, *An Attempt to Explain God's Gracious Covenant with Believers; and Illustrate the Duty of Parents to Embrace This Covenant, Dedicate Their Children in Baptism and Train Them Up in the Fear of God* (Amherst, NH: Joseph Cushing, 1805); John Reed, *An Apology for the Rite of Infant Baptism, and for the Usual Modes of Baptizing* (Providence: Heaton & Williams, 1806); Nathaniel S. Prime, *A Familiar Illustration of Christian Baptism: in Which the Proper Subjects of that Ordinance and the Mode of Administration are Ascertained* (Salem, NY: Dodd & Stevenson, 1818); Charles Jerram, *Conversations on Infant Baptism* (New York: Swords, Stanford, & Co., 1839); Alexander Hay, *A Treatise on Baptism* (New York: J.A. Sparks, 1842); William Goode, *The Doctrine of the Church of England as to the Effects of Baptism in the Case of Infants* (London: J. Hatchard and Son, 1850); Thomas M'Crie, *Lectures on Christian Baptism* (Edinburgh: Johnstone & Hunter, 1850); William Sommerville, *A Dissertation on the Nature and Administration of the Ordinance of Baptism* (Edinburgh: Oliver & Boyd, 1866); E. Greenwald, *The Baptism of Children* (Philadelphia: Sherman, 1872); N. Doane, *Infant Baptism Briefly Considered* (New

York: Nelson & Phillips, 1875); J.W. Etter, *The Doctrine of Christian Baptism* (Dayton, OH: United Brethren Press, 1888).

Twentieth Century

Lewis Bevens Schenck, *The Presbyterian Doctrine of Children in the Covenant: An Historical Study of the Significance of Infant Baptism in the Presbyterian Church in America* (New Haven: Yale University Press, 1940); Raymond R. Van Heukelom, "The Meaning of Baptism in Reformed Theology" (Th.M. thesis, Calvin Theological Seminary, 1943); W. H. Flemington, *The New Testament Doctrine of Baptism* (London: S.P.C.K., 1953); Pierre Ch. Marcel, *The Biblical Doctrine of Infant Baptism: Sacrament of the Covenant of Grace* (London: James Clark, 1953); Geoffrey W. Bromiley, *Baptism and the Anglican Reformers* (London: S.P.C.K., 1953); M. Eugene Osterhaven, *What is Christian Baptism?* (Grand Rapids: Society for Reformed Publications, 1956); Robert G. Rayburn, *What About Baptism?* (St. Louis: Covenant Theological Seminary, 1957); Dwight Hervey Small, *The Biblical Basis for Infant Baptism: Children in God's Covenant Promises* (Westwood, NJ: Revell, 1959); Joachim Jeremias, *Infant Baptism in the First Four Centuries*, translated by David Cairns (Philadelphia: Westminster Press, 1962); J.G. Vos, *Baptism: Its Subjects and Modes* (Pittsburgh, PA: Crown and Covenant Publications, 1969); John A. Schep, *Baptism in the Spirit According to Scripture* (Plainfield, NJ: Logos International, 1972); John Murray, *Christian Baptism* (Grand Rapids: Baker, 1974); Jay E. Adams, *Meaning and Mode of Baptism* (Philipsburg, NJ: Presbyterian and Reformed, 1976); Francis A. Schaeffer, *Baptism* (Wilmington, DE: Trimark, 1976); Wilbert M. Van Dyk, "'Forbid Them Not': A Study in Infant Baptism" (Th.M. thesis, Calvin Theological Seminary, 1976); Robert K. Churchill, *Glorious is the Baptism of the Spirit* (Philipsburg, NJ: Presbyterian and Reformed, 1976); Edmund B. Fairfield, *Letters on Baptism* (Uxbridge, MA: Reformation Seminary Press, 1979); Geoffrey W. Bromiley, *Children of Promise: The Case for Baptizing Infants* (Grand Rapids: Eerdmans, 1979); Willem Balke, *Calvin and the Anabaptist Radicals,* translated by William Heynen (Grand Rapids: Eerdmans, 1981); Samuel Miller, *Baptism and Christian Education* (reprint Dallas, TX: Presbyterian Heritage Publications, 1984); Duane E. Spencer, *Holy Baptism: Word Keys Which Unlock the Covenant* (Tyler, TX: Geneva Ministries, 1984); James W. Dale, *Classic Baptism: An Inquiry into the Meaning of the Word as Determined by the Usage of*

Classical Greek Writers (Philipsburg, NJ: Presbyterian and Reformed, 1989); H. Oliphant Old, *The Shaping of the Reformed Baptismal Rite in the Sixteenth Century* (Grand Rapids: Eerdmans, 1990); Jonathan Neil Gerstner, *The Thousand Generation Covenant: Dutch Reformed Covenant Theology and Group Identity in Colonial South Africa, 1652-1854* (Leiden: E.J. Brill, 1991); Rowland S. Ward, *Baptism in Scripture and History* (Brunswick, Australia: Globe Press, 1991); Frederick S. Leahy, *Biblical Baptism* (Belfast: Cameron Press, 1992); Robert R. Booth, *Children of the Promise: The Biblical Case for Infant Baptism* (Philipsburg, NJ: Presbyterian and Reformed, 1995); Robert Grossmann, *The Meaning and Administration of Biblical Baptism* (Garner, IA: Elector, 1995); Gerald Procee, *Holy Baptism: The Scriptural Setting, Significance and Scope of Infant Baptism* (Hamilton, Ontario: Free Reformed Church, 1998).

ARTICLE 35

The Holy Supper

Some of the best works on the Lord's Supper include:

Seventeenth Century

Simon Patrick, *Mensa Mystica, or a Discourse Concerning the Sacrament of the Lord's Supper* (London: Francis Tyton, 1676); Simon Patrick, *The Christian Sacrifice: A Treatise Shewing the Necessity, End and Manner of Receiving the Holy Communion* (London: R. Royston, 1679).

Eighteenth Century

Jabez Earl, *Sacramental Exercises in Two Parts: The Christian's Employment before, at, and after the Lord's Supper; and The Christian's Conduct in his Afterlife* (London: Richard Hett, 1742); W. Fleetwood, *The Reasonable Communicant: Or, An Explanation of the Doctrine of the Sacrament of the Lord's Supper* (London: John, Francis, and Charles Rivington, 1784).

Nineteenth Century

John Warden, *A Practical Essay on the Lord's Supper to which is Added an Assistant in Examining the Heart; or Questions of the Greatest Moment, which Every Christian Ought, with Sincerity, and as in the Sight of God, to Put to his own Heart* (Leith: Archibald Allardice and W. Coke, 1809); Thomas Haweis, *The Communicant's Spiritual Companion; or, An Evangelical Preparation for the Lord's Supper* (New Haven: Oliver Steele, 1810); Henry Grove, *A Discourse Concerning the Nature and Design of the Lord's Supper* (Salem, NY: Joshua Cushing, 1812); John Willison, *A Sacramental Directory; or a Treatise Concerning the Sanctification of a Communion-Sabbath* (Edinburgh: Ogle, Allardice, & Thomson, 1817); Hugh Blair, *A Companion to the Altar; Shewing the Nature and Necessity of a Sacramental Preparation in Order to our Worthy Receiving the Holy Communion* (London: Scatcherd and Letterman, 1820); Edward Bickersteth, *A Treatise on the Lord's Supper: Designed as a Guide and Companion to the Holy Communion* (London: R.B. Seeley and W. Burnside, 1830); Capel Molyneux, *The Lord's Supper* (London: James Nisbet, 1850); James W. Alexander, *Plain Words to a Young Communicant* (New York: Anson D.F. Randolph, 1858); Samuel Luckey, *The Lord's Supper* (New York: Carlton & Porter, 1859); Matthew Henry, *The Communicant's Companion; or, Instructions for the Right Receiving of the Lord's Supper* (Philadelphia: Presbyterian Board of Publication, 1865); Thomas Houston, *The Lord's Supper: its Nature, Ends, and Obligation; and Mode of Administration* (Edinburgh: James Gemmell, 1878); John Glas, *A Treatise on the Lord's Supper* (London: Sampson Low, et al., 1883); Nicholas Ridley, *A Brief Declaration of the Lord's Supper*, ed. H.C.G. Moule (London: Seeley, 1895).

Twentieth Century
W. Mason, *The Christian Communicant; or a Suitable Companion to the Lord's Supper* (London: Chas. J. Thynne, 1904); Robert Bruce, *The Mystery of the Lord's Supper*, edited by Thomas F. Torrance (London: James Clarke, 1958); Ernest F. Kevan, *The Lord's Supper* (London: Evangelical Press, 1966); Joachim Jeremias, *The Eucharistic Words of Jesus*, translated by Norman Perrin (London: SCM, 1966); Gerard Wisse, *May I Partake of the Lord's Supper?* (Wilmington, DE: Trimark, 1979); Richard Bacon, *What Mean ye by This Service? Paedocommunion in Light of the Passover* (Texas: Presbyterian Heritage Publications, 1989); John Willison, *Meditations on the Lord's Supper* (abridged reprint Stornoway: Reformation Press, 1990).

Historical-Theological Studies
Numerous historical-theological studies have been undertaken on the Reformation view of the Lord's Supper. Alexander Barclay, *The Protestant Doctrine of the Lord's Supper* (Glasgow, 1927), shows the affinity between Luther and Calvin but regards Calvin's doctrine as the natural development of Zwingli's later thinking on the Lord's Supper. Cyril C. Richardson, *Zwingli and Cranmer on the Eucharist* (Evanston, IL, 1949) asserts that Cranmer did not move beyond the Zwinglian framework. Joseph C. McLelland, *The Visible Words of God: An Exposition of the Sacramental Theology of Peter Martyr Vermigli* (Grand Rapids: Eerdmans, 1957) establishes the theological harmony between Vermigli, Bucer, and Calvin on the Holy Supper.

George B. Burnet, *The Holy Communion in the Reformed Church of Scotland 1560-1960* (London: Oliver & Boyd, 1960) reveals the rich Scottish heritage on Communion. Peter Newman Brooks, *Thomas Cranmer's Doctrine of the Eucharist* (New York: Seabury Press, 1965) argues that Cranmer held much the same doctrine of a "true presence" of Christ in the supper as did Bucer, Bullinger, and Calvin. Leigh Eric Schmidt, *Holy Fair: Scottish Communions and American Revivals in the Early Modern Period* (Princeton: University Press, 1989) explores the historical development of the Scottish communion season from the Reformation to the nineteenth century, documents its extension to colonial America and its important relationship to revivals on both sides of the Atlantic. Brian A. Gerrish, *Grace and Gratitude: The Eucharistic Theology of John Calvin* (Minneapolis: Fortress Press, 1993) puts Calvin's doctrine of the Lord's Supper in the context of his theology as a whole, and compares him with Zwingli and Luther.

ARTICLE 36

Church and State

The most informative research tool on church-state relations is Albert J. Menendez, *Church-State Relations: An Annotated Bibliography* (New York: Garland, 1976). Menendez, however, includes only English language, full-length books that treat the subject in some depth or completeness.

The classic Christian work on church and state is Augustine's *City of God,* translated by Marcus Dods (New York: Random House, 1952). For an able exposition of Augustine's ideas, see John H.S. Burleigh, *The City of God: A Study of St. Augustine's Philosophy* (London: Nisbet, 1949); also, consult James Boice, *Two Cities, Two Loves* (Downers Grove, IL: InterVarsity, 1996). See Claudio Morino, *Church and State in the Teaching of St. Ambrose,* translated by M. Joseph Costelloe (Washington, D.C.: Catholic University of America, 1969), for information on another ancient churchman who dealt with church-state relations.

For medieval thought on church-state relations, see Heinrich A. Rommen, *The State in Catholic Thought* (St. Louis: B. Herder, 1947); Arthur L. Smith, *Church and State in the Middle Ages* (New York: Barnes & Noble, 1964); Brian Tierney, *The Crisis of Church and State, 1050-1300* (Englewood Cliffs, NJ: Prentice-Hall, 1966); Bennett D. Hill, *Church and State in the Middle Ages* (New York: Wiley, 1970); Thomas J. Renna, *Church and State in Medieval Europe, 1050-1314* (Dubuque, IA: Kendall/Hunt, 1974). Also, consult Thomas Aquinas, *Compendium of Theology,* translated by C.O. Vollert (London: Herder, 1948).

For pre-Reformation thinking on church and state, see *The English Works of John Wyclif,* 3 vols., edited by F.D. Matthews (London: Wyclif Society, 1880); John Hus, *The Church,* translated by David Schaff (New York: Scribners, 1915). For Reformation thought, consult H.R. Pearcy, *The Meaning of the Church in the Thought of Calvin* (Chicago: University Press, 1941); William A. Mueller, *Church and State in Luther and Calvin* (Nashville: Broadman, 1954); Thomas F. Torrance, *Kingdom and Church* (Edinburgh: Oliver and Boyd, 1956); Geddes MacGregor, *Corpus Christi: The Nature of the Church According to the Reformed Tradition* (Philadelphia: Westminster, 1958); John Tonkin, *The Church and the Secular Order in Reformation Thought* (New York: Columbia University Press, 1971). For the Anabaptist view, see John Toews, "The Anabaptist Conception of the Church" (Ph.D. dissertation, United College of Winnipeg, 1950); Franklin H. Littell, *The Anabaptist View of the Church* (Boston: Beacon Press, 1952), which was revised and reissued as *The Origins of Sectarian Protestantism* (New York: Macmillan, 1965).

Numerous treatises have been written on church-state relations in the United Kingdom. For Scotland, see the *First Book of Discipline* (1560); the *Second Book of Discipline* (1578); Samuel Rutherford, *Lex Rex, or The Law and the Prince* (1644; reprint Harrisonburg, VA: Sprinkle, 1982), and *A Free Disputation Against Pretended Liberty of Conscience* (London: R.I. for Andrew Crook, 1649); George Gillespie, *Aaron's Rod Blossoming; or, The Divine Ordinance of Church Government Vindicated* (1646; reprint Harrisonburg, VA: Sprinkle, 1985); Thomas Brown, *Church and State in Scotland* (Edinburgh: Macniven and Wallace, 1891); Francis Lyall, *Of Presbyters and Kings: Church and State in the Law of Scotland* (Aberdeen: University Press, 1980). For England, see Gilbert W. Child, *Church and State Under the Tudors* (London: Longmans, 1890); Henry M. Gwatkin, *Church and State in England to the Death of Queen Anne* (London: Longmans, 1917); A.F. Scott Pearson, *Church and State: Political Aspects of Sixteenth Century Puritanism* (Cambridge: University Press, 1928); Adrian Hastings, *Church and State: The English Experience* (Exeter: University Press, 1991); Stuart E. Prull, *Church and State in Tudor and Stuart England* (Arlington Heights, IL: H. Davidson, 1993).

For church-state relations in Europe, consult William Graham, *A Review of Ecclesiastical Establishments in Europe* (Glasgow: D. Niven, 1792); H. Geffcken, *Church and State: Their Relations Historically Considered* (London, 1852); Adolf Keller, *Church and State on the European Continent, 1864-1914* (London: Epworth, 1936); Ernst C. Helmreich, ed., *Church and State in Europe* (St. Louis: Focrum Press, 1979).

For church-state relations in America, the best resource is John

F. Wilson, ed., *Church and State in America: A Bibliographical Guide*, 2 vols. (New York: Greenwood Press, 1986-87). Volume 1 covers the colonial and early national periods; Volume 2, from the civil war to the 1980s. Each volume has eleven bibliographic essays, with approximately 250 entries each. For specific works, see Joseph P. Thompson, *Church and State in the United States* (Boston: James R. Osgood, 1873); Philip Schaff, *Church and State in the United States* (New York: G.P. Putnam's Sons, 1888); William A. Brown, *Church and State in Contemporary America* (New York: Scribners, 1936); Anson P. Stokes, *Church and State in the United States,* 3 vols. (New York: Harper, 1950); James E. Wood, Jr., ed., *Religion and the State* (Waco, TX: Baylor University Press, 1985).

For church-state relations in general, see William E. Gladstone, *The State in Its Relations to the Church* (London: J. Murray, 1841); Samuel Taylor Coleridge, *On the Constitution of Church and State,* edited by John Colmer (1852; reprint London: Routledge & Kegan, 1976); Albert Hyma, *Christianity and Politics: A History of the Principles and Struggles of Church and State* (Philadelphia: Lippincott, 1938); Luigi Sturzo, *Church and State,* 2 vols., translated by B.B. Carter (1939; reprint Notre Dame, IN: University Press, 1962); Finley M. Foster, *Church and State: Their Relations Considered* (New York: Peerless, 1940); G. Elson Rupp, *The Dilemma of Church and State* (Philadelphia: Muhlenberg, 1954); Jacob Marcellus Kik, *Church and State: The Story of Two Kingdoms* (New York: Nelson, 1963); Albert G. Huegli, *Church and State Under God* (St. Louis: Concordia, 1964); Thomas Sanders, *Protestant Concepts of Church and State* (New York: Holt, Rinehart, and Winston, 1964).

ARTICLE 37

The Last Judgment; Hell and Heaven

For helpful material on the last judgment, hell and heaven, and eschatology in general, consult the great Reformed orthodox systematicians as well as Reformed commentators on the book of Revelation, such as James B. Ramsay, *Revelation* (1873; reprint Edinburgh: Banner of Truth Trust, 1977); William Hendriksen, *More Than Conquerors* (Grand Rapids: Baker, 1939); Herman Hoeksema, *Behold He Cometh!* (Grand Rapids: Reformed Free, 1969); Philip E. Hughes, *Revelation* (Grand Rapids: Eerdmans, 1990).

Seventeenth Century

The Puritans wrote extensively on what they called "the four last things": death, judgment, heaven, and hell (e.g., Robert Bolton, *The Four Last Things* [1633; reprint Pittsburgh: Soli Deo Gloria, 1990]; William Bates, "The Four Last Things" [1691] in *Complete Works,* ed. W. Farmer [reprint Harrisonburg, VA: Sprinkle, 1990], 3:237-507, which is probably Bates's greatest work). The greatest and most massive Puritan classic on heaven is Richard Baxter, *The Saints' Everlasting Rest* (1650; reprinted often in abridged versions, e.g. Grand Rapids: Zondervan, 1962). For the doctrine of man's soul in the face of eternity, see John Flavel, "Pneumatologia: A Treatise of the Soul of Man," in *The Works* (reprint London: Banner of Truth Trust, 1968), 2:475-609, 3:1-238.

Eighteenth Century

The greatest eighteenth-century classic on man's eternal abode is Isaac Watts, *The World to Come* (1739; reprint Chicago: Moody, 1954). For moving and searching sermons on "the last things" that no preacher has ever surpassed, see Jonathan Edwards (a variety of sermons in *The Works,* Vol. 2 [reprint Edinburgh: Banner of Truth Trust, 1974]). Some of those sermons have been reprinted in Jonathan Edwards, *The Wrath of Almighty God* (Morgan, PA: Soli Deo Gloria, 1996). For Edwards's views, see John H. Gerstner, *Jonathan Edwards on Heaven and Hell* (Grand Rapids: Baker, 1980).

Nineteenth Century

The best nineteenth-century works are Wilson C. Rider, *A Course of Lectures on Future Punishment* (Ellsworth: Daniel T. Pike, 1836); J. Edmondson, *Scripture Views of the Heavenly World* (New York: Lane & Scott, 1852); W.G.T. Shedd, *The Doctrine of Endless Punishment* (1885; reprint Edinburgh: Banner of Truth Trust, 1986).

Twentieth Century

Helpful twentieth-century theological treatises on various aspects of eschatology include Geerhardus Vos, *The Pauline Eschatology* (1930; reprint Grand Rapids: Baker, 1979); Diedrich H. Kromminga, *The Millennium in the Church: Studies in the History of Christian Chiliasm* (Grand Rapids: Eerdmans, 1945); Klaas Schilder, *Heaven: What Is It?* (Grand Rapids: Eerdmans, 1950); Louis Berkhof, *The Second Coming of Christ* (Grand Rapids: Eerdmans, 1952); Harry Buis, *The Doctrine of Eternal Punishment* (Grand Rapids: Baker, 1957); Loraine Boettner, *Immortality* (Philadelphia: Presbyterian and Reformed, 1958); Leon Morris, *The Biblical Doctrine of Judgment* (London: Tyndale Press, 1960); Herman N. Ridderbos, *The Coming of the Kingdom* (Philadelphia: Presbyterian and Reformed, 1962); Bernard Ramm, *Them He Glorified: A Systematic Study of the Doctrine of Glorification* (Grand Rapids: Eerdmans, 1963); Oswald T. Allis, *Prophecy and the Church* (Philadelphia: Presbyterian and Reformed, 1964); Jay E. Adams, *I Tell You the Mystery* (Lookout Mountain, TX: Prospective Press, 1966); Wilbur M. Smith, *The Biblical Doctrine of Heaven* (Chicago: Moody, 1968); George L. Murray, *Millennial Studies: A Search for Truth* (Grand Rapids: Baker, 1972); Gerrit C. Berkouwer, *The Return of Christ,* translated by James VanOosterom (Grand Rapids: Eerdmans, 1972); Philip E. Hughes, *Interpreting Prophecy: An Essay in Biblical Perspectives* (Grand Rapids: Eerdmans, 1976); Leslie H. Woodson, *What the Bible Says About Hell* (Grand Rapids: Baker, 1976); Anthony A. Hoekema, *The Bible and the Future* (Grand Rapids: Eerdmans, 1979); Stephen Travis, *I Believe in the Second Coming of Jesus* (Grand Rapids: Eerdmans, 1982); Robert A.

Morey, *Death and the Afterlife* (Minneapolis: Bethany, 1984); Eryl Davies, *The Wrath of God* (Mid-Glamorgan, Wales: Evangelical Press of Wales, 1984); Peter Toon, *Heaven and Hell: A Biblical and Theological Overview* (Nashville: Nelson, 1986); John Gilmore, *Probing Heaven: Key Questions on the Hereafter* (Grand Rapids: Baker, 1989); Paul Helm, *The Last Things: Death, Judgment, Heaven, Hell* (Edinburgh: Banner of Truth Trust, 1989); John H. Gerstner, *Repent or Perish: With a Special Reference to the Conservative Attack on Hell* (Ligonier, PA: Soli Deo Gloria, 1990); John MacArthur, *The Glory of Heaven* (Wheaton, IL: Crossway, 1996); Herman Bavinck, *The Last Things: Hope for This World and the Next*, edited by John Bolt, translated by John Vriend (Grand Rapids: Baker, 1996).

For twentieth-century historical-theological studies, see Heinrich Quistorp, *Calvin's Doctrine of the Last Things*, translated by Harold Knight (London: Lutterworth Press, 1955); D.P. Walker, *The Decline of Hell: Seventeenth-Century Discussions of Eternal Torment* (Chicago: University Press, 1964); J. A. Mourant, *Augustine on Immortality* (Philadelphia: Villanova University Press, 1969); Peter Toon, *The Puritans, the Millennium, and the Future of Israel* (London: James Clarke, 1970); Iain Murray, *The Puritan Hope: A Study of Renewal and the Interpretation of Prophecy* (London: Banner of Truth Trust, 1971); Timothy P. Weber, *Living in the Shadow of the Second Coming: American Premillennialism, 1879-1925* (New York: Oxford University Press, 1979); Colleen McDannell and Bernhard Long, *Heaven: A History* (New Haven, CT: Yale University Press, 1988); B.E. Daley, *The Hope of the Early Church: Eschatology in the Patristic Age* (Cambridge: University Press, 1991).

Where should you begin? Read the book of Revelation again. While doing so, consult Herman Hoeksema's *Behold He Cometh*. Then read Paul Helm's *The Last Things*, followed by Anthony Hoekema's *The Bible and the Future*, and Herman Bavinck's *The Last Things*.

Sources for Reformed Literature

New Books Offered at Discount Prices

Audubon Press
3515 Audubon Drive
P.O. Box 8055
Laurel, MS 39441-8000

Bible Truth Books
P.O. Box 2373
Kalamazoo, MI 49003

Christian Book Distributors
P.O. Box 7000
Peabody, MA 01961-7000

Cumberland Valley Bible Book Service
133 North Hanover Street
P.O. Box 613
Carlisle, PA 17013

Gospel Mission
P.O. Box 318
Choteau, MT 59422

Great Christian Books
229 South Bridge Street
P.O. Box 8000
Elkton, MD 21922-8000

Reformation Heritage Books
2919 Leonard NE
Grand Rapids, MI 49525

Still Waters Revival Books
4710-37 A Ave.
Edmonton, AB Canada
T6L 3T5

Trinity Book Service
P.O. Box 395
Montville, NJ 07045

Westminster Discount Book Service
P.O. Box 125-H
Scarsdale, NY 10583

Used Books

Academy Books
13 Marmion Road
Southsea, Hantshire, PO5 2AT
England

Antiquarian Books
David C. Lachman
127 Woodland Road
Wyncote, PA 19095

Baker Book House
P.O. Box 6287
Grand Rapids, MI 49546

**Dickson Books, James A.
Christian Bookshop**
12 Forrest Road
Edinburgh EH1 2QN
Scotland

Annotated Bibliography

Drummond, James
31 Argyll View
Larne, County Antrim,
North Ireland

Ex Libris Theological Books
P.O. Box 810
Oak Lawn, IL 60454

Family Book Services
826 Edna St., S.E.
Grand Rapids, MI 49507

Foundation Books
P.O. Box 7086
Roanoake, VA 24019

Geneva Books
58 Elms Road
London SW4 9EW
England

Good Books
Curt Daniel
2456 Devonshire Rd.
Springfield, IL 62703

Gowan Books, John
Drumaraw
Springfield
Enniskillen
North Ireland

Humber Books
Rozel House, 4 St. Marys Lane
Barton-on-Humber DN18 5EX
South Humberside, England

Kregel Publications
P.O. Box 2607
Grand Rapids, MI 59401-2607

Nelson's Bookroom
Lydbury North
Shropshire, SY7 8AS
England

Peek, G.
Fairfields, Chapel Road, Beighton
Norwich, NR13 3LF
England

Pendlebury's Bookshop
Church House, Portland Ave.
Stamford Hill, London N16 6HJ
England

Reformation Heritage Books
2919 Leonard NE
Grand Rapids, MI 49525

Roberts, Richard Owens
Box 21
Wheaton, IL 60189

The Theological Antiquarian
5 Wildwood Dr.
East Haven, CT 06512